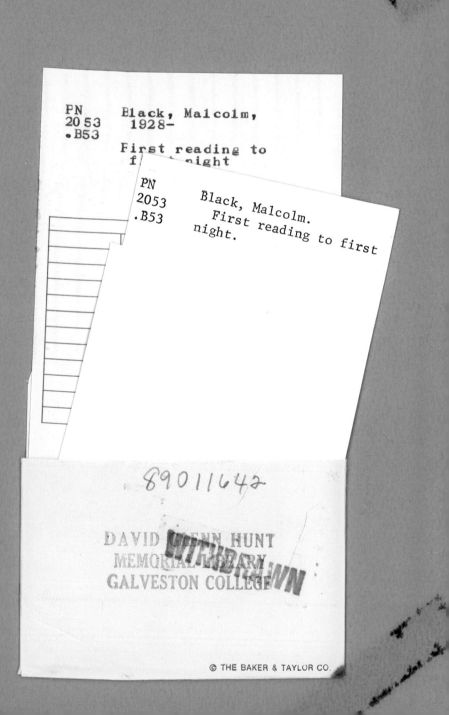

FIRST READING TO FIRST NIGHT

FIRST READING TO FIRST NIGHT

A Candid Look at Stage Directing

MALCOLM BLACK

UNIVERSITY OF WASHINGTON PRESS

Seattle and London

Library of Congress Cataloging in Publication Data

Black, Malcolm, 1928-
   First reading to first night.

   1. Theater—Production and direction.   I. Title.
PN2053.B53   792'.0233   75-20336
ISBN 0-295-95432-9

This book is for my eldest son, Duncan, in the hope that it will help him to understand where I was most of the time.

Acknowledgments

I wish to thank, in alphabetical order, the audiences, composers, designers, performers, producers, stage crews, stage managers, students, writers, and many others who have enabled me to be a director.

I wish to acknowledge the critics, designers, and photographers whose work is reproduced here. Their names are listed by the appropriate items.

Gordon Gould has not only given fine performances in plays I have directed; he also gave me, in abundance, the benefit of his literary experience, for which I thank him.

This book would never have been started, let alone finished, had it not been for my wife, Charla, to whom I owed so much already.

Malcolm Black

Introduction

The other day I was talking to an actress friend of mine about a new book of theatrical criticism. She interrupted my enthusiastic comments by saying: ''But we just don't have enough theater in this country for all the writing that's going on.'' I cannot disagree with her. There is far more writing about theater, studying of theater, and training for theater in the United States than there is actual theater, and this disproportion is increasing every year. This is, of course, merely a lead-in to the question: Why write *another* book on the subject?

There are already many books on directing, and some of them are very interesting. They range from the rigid rule books and manuals to the autobiographies of leading practitioners of the craft, who invariably give fascinating, if somewhat subjective, accounts of their more spectacular successes. I do not know of a book, however, that deals honestly with the day-to-day realities of being a stage director. Many authors have described what they think should happen; I am going to try to trace, realistically rather than theoretically, the progression of a director's work from his first exposure to the script to the opening night.

When I was working full time in regional theater, community organizations and cultural groups frequently asked me to talk about my work. Also, I have taught directing courses in two major universities and had many good talks with people who wanted to direct. This book is actually the result of these encounters.

Although I have chosen to deal primarily with the professional theater, the facts are applicable to all situations, and I hope this book will be of interest to students of theater and directors in schools and community drama groups. As it is not intended as a textbook, but rather the "credo" of one director, I also hope that it will interest people whose connection with the theater is primarily as members of the audience.

An autobiography is certainly the last thing I wish to get into, but I feel that I should give a few details of my background, even if only to explain some of my obvious prejudices. I was born in Liverpool, England, in 1928 and had the normal education of a middle-class English male: sexually segregated boarding schools from early childhood culminating in obligatory military service. On my release from the British army, an event that was of immense benefit to both parties, I was lucky enough to obtain a scholarship to the Old Vic School in London. My principal mentors there were Michel Saint-Denis, Glen Byam Shaw, George Devine, and John Blatchley. One could say I started right at the top.

After free-lancing as a stage manager and an actor, I joined the production staff of the BBC. Wishing to broaden my somewhat narrow horizon, I went to Canada in 1956 and spent three years at Toronto's Crest Theatre, leaving there to join the American Shakespeare Festival in Stratford, Connecticut. Since 1961 I have directed productions all over the United States and Canada. Included in this period was a wonderful six-year association with the Playhouse Theatre Company of Vancouver, British Columbia. For three of these years I was the theater's artistic director.

In 1968 I received a totally unexpected telephone call from Gregory A. Falls of the University of Washington, inviting me to be visiting professor in directing. I was as intrigued as I was surprised by the prospect, and I accepted his offer. And since that time I have combined the life of the university with that of the professional theater, so I may now be said to qualify as both "poet and pedant."

Contents

Illustrations

FIRST READING TO FIRST NIGHT

First Reading
of the Script

In the beginning is the word. All good productions begin with something on paper. It may be a full-length masterpiece, a commedia dell'arte scenario, or even a "treatment" for an idea. Let us assume for our purposes that it is a full-length play.

In studying a play there are usually three phases: the first impressions upon reading the script; the more detailed exploration, which includes the first meetings with designers and casting people; and the in-depth prerehearsal work, when the show has been designed and cast.

FIRST IMPRESSIONS

The most important contact that a director has with a script is his first one. It is the only time he can be totally objective and experience the material with the same freshness as an audience. By the time a director has read the play twice, he is ahead of the public. He has clarified for himself whatever problems in the plot line that he noticed the first time around. The theater patron, on the other hand, is not likely to come back in search of clarification.

The normal procedure begins with a call from your agent, who says: "Irving Smith is doing a new play, and I have submitted your name." When you get to meet Irving, he usually starts by telling you why he asked for you. (Just remember that agents like to be creative, too!) There is always great urgency on these occasions, and the script is invariably sent over by a special messenger.

Before you even unwrap it, your agent is on the phone asking how you like it and telling you to read it immediately because the producer is waiting to talk with you. Unless you are a very independent director (a rare breed in these days of theatrical recession), you will invariably find yourself discussing the play after only cursory study. If your first reading has followed the procedure as I am going to suggest, you are more likely to get off on the right footing with your producer.

Thus, when a script arrives for a director's consideration, there is always a temptation to pick it up immediately and start reading, even if you are about to leave for an appointment. But you cannot give a play a satisfactory first reading if you have to do it in dribs and drabs on the subway or between the eggs and breakfast toast. It is much better to put off the reading until you have time to give it full attention and to prepare properly for what is an important occasion.

If you live alone, take the phone off the hook. If you do not, then arrange for your spouse, or whoever, to answer it. Get a substantial pad of paper and something to write with. If the playwright begins with a description of the set, particularly if the play is a farce or a mystery where the layout is most important, sketch out his floor plan so that as you read you will have a visual reminder of the topography he had envisioned. Every time you have a question or a doubt, write it down. These notes are invaluable and you should keep them right through final rehearsals, so that you can continue asking yourself the questions you asked before you knew the play. By doing this you can be certain you have tried to make crystal clear those moments that seemed confusing during your first reading.

At the risk of sounding dogmatic on this subject, I should add that I believe it even helps if you do not take a break in your reading until the end of a scene. The more you can imagine yourself as a potential audience member, the better you can record those invaluable first impressions.

I once directed a very funny new farce. On my first reading, two of the most amusing scenes seemed unnecessary to the story line. I asked the author about them, and he gave me excellent reasons for their existence. Some time later, I directed a revival of the play, and at the preview I was struck again by the redundance of these scenes. This time the author was not around to justify their existence, and I was right back to my original impression. Although the Dramatists' Guild (the playwrights' professional organization) gives the author, contractually, the final say in everything, I should, at least, have shown the writer a run-through with the two scenes deleted.

If you are reading a musical script, you should have the score in front of you, because the music is an integral part of the whole work. If you cannot read a score, then get a tape of the music or, in the case of a revival, the record album, and play the songs as they occur.

Even if the play you are considering is one that you have previously read or seen, your first reading from the director's point of view is still crucial. Once you have done a few plays, you automatically think of the piece on the stage as you read it. There is a difference between hypothetical notions and the knowledge that you may be guiding the work yourself in a few weeks!

The recording of first impressions has a twofold purpose. The obvious one is that it marks the beginning of the creative work. The second concerns the less-than-ideal realities of the director's profession.

FINDING A "HANDLE"

The best thing that can happen in the early stages of study is to find a "handle" for the play ("concept" is really too fancy a word at this stage). For example, the first time I read *Philadelphia, Here I Come*, I was immediately attracted to the play. However, the device of having the alter ego of one of the principal characters, Gar, appear on stage as Private presents certain stylistic problems. Right at the end of the play, Private Gar says to Public Gar: "Watch her carefully, every moment, every gesture, every little peculiarity: Keep the camera whirring; for this is a film you'll run over and over again—Madge Going to Bed On My Last Night At Home . . . Madge. . . . " As I read this, it suddenly hit me that the whole play could be the running of that film, a series of flashbacks of that fateful evening. I reread the play from that point of view and felt secure about the "handle." The designer Charles Evans and I later worked out a scenic concept whereby only the items used, the most vivid in Gar's memory, were on the stage. They were all very positive: the kitchen table to end all kitchen tables; an indelible rug beside Gar's bed. Everything not used or referred to was completely neutral. The final production was one of the few I have done with which I was totally satisfied. Everything just fell into place (see fig. 1).

The danger of trying to arrive at an approach too quickly, after only superficial study, is that you may arrive at the wrong one. Then, when you have really come to terms with a play, a completely different approach may present itself. Even when forced into hasty decisions just to get hired, I have always tried to delay the design meetings as long as possible. But there is seldom enough time. Even within the halls of ivy, you can be pressured to make decisions too soon. So the dangers I am writing about are applicable on campus as well as in the marketplace.

Producers

Many people have defined the responsibilities of a director, but such lists of duties tend to describe the ideal. In fact, the director's function varies in every situation. At one extreme is the high school director, who is likely to be responsible for everything from the choice of the play to the printing of tickets. At the other extreme is the stage director in the average opera company. As the prima donnas, of all sexes, arrive at the last minute, he can do little more than show them where the entrances are and keep the chorus out of their way. As if being relegated to the position of traffic cop were not bad enough, he can not even smoke at the rehearsals because it is bad for the singers' throats.

THE ROLE OF THE PRODUCER

It will be easier to discuss some of the different situations that a director may encounter if we first examine the functions of the producer, for in the professional theater it is the producer who engages the director. Further, if the production is a new play, the author must approve the producer's choice; but the extent to which the author exercises this power of approval will depend entirely on the amount of confidence he feels in the strength of his position. The producer is also responsible for raising the money to finance the production, and he will normally supervise the marketing of the product. There are many producers who do no more than this, although they would be loath to admit it. If you ask a producer what he considers to be his job (as I have done), he will probably come up with something like: "A producer is the man who welds the creative elements together."

I once did a production for which one of the producers was the late Lawrence (Jimmy) Carr. We were talking about flops (an appropriate subject for this particular show), and he said, "Even though I've had my failures, I've always been able to walk into Sardi's with my head held high" (Sardi's is New York City's leading theatrical restaurant). I found this a most revealing and in a way rather touching insight into the mind of a leading Broadway producer.

THE FIRST MEETING BETWEEN PRODUCER AND DIRECTOR

But I digress. Let us assume that the script has been read, albeit rather cursorily, and I am about to meet the producer. I believe the art of these meetings (they are often the director's equivalent of an audition) is to get the people who have sent for you to do as much of the talking as possible. (With theater people this is not difficult!) If you can limit your comments to the few things you are certain about, you will be in better shape. I know this sounds obvious, but it is amazing how often one gets led into all kinds of premature decisions by overanxious and overenthusiastic producers who are frequently many months away from production and thousands of dollars short of the money needed to produce.

THE POWER STRUGGLE

The theater on every level is really an appalling power struggle. Contractually the director's rights are negligible, unless he is someone like Bob Fosse or Mike Nichols, so he must therefore establish his position from the beginning. He has to be able to assess the people he is dealing with, however, and be realistic about the amount of give and take that will be necessary for a good working relationship. If you are a new director, and you are meeting with top-echelon producers and playwrights, you are going to have to wield your authority with a good deal of tact, but on the other hand, the help you get from them will be considerable.

There are other situations where you are clearly far more experienced than the people who are interviewing you and you are immediately and incontestably at the helm when you accept the assignment. If you are meeting with producers who have a script that interests you but about which you have many reservations, then you had better be frank with them—especially if they think they have a masterpiece on their hands. If your views are clearly not making any impression on them, now is the time to bow out. It is amazing how the less enthusiastic you are at these meetings, the more they seem to want you.

At this first meeting it is essential to try to find out what kind of a budget a producer is proposing. A director must have some knowledge of costs. If your preliminary readings have convinced you that only a turntable will make an episodic play workable, there is no point in pursuing the project unless the producer will spend that kind of money.

The reason I have referred to the power struggle of the theater is that it is built into the system and you will always have to contend with it. Like most directors, I like to do my own casting and choose my own designers, composers, and stage managers. I am not power hungry; I simply believe a production is better served when the director picks his own people. Nobody can know better than the director the kind of artists with whom he can have the rapport necessary for a good production. When you are starting out, it can be a real battle to secure the right to make all these decisions. As you become established and know that you are in a strong bargaining position with a producer, you can insist on your choices or refuse the job.

The producer's point of view, and it is a valid one, is that if he is just going to be the "money man," he is not interested in producing. What usually happens is that the director ends up bargaining: he gets his choreographer, but agrees to take the character man who had been the producer's lover when they were in Drama School together.

The ideal situation would be one in which the director had complete respect for the producer and could use him as a sounding board for his own ideas. There are such producers, but they are few and far between. I have also worked for those who made Zero Mostel in the movie, *The Producers*, appear to be underplaying.

The first time I worked for an "important" producer was in

stock. My agent encouraged me to take a ridiculously small fee because the theater was "prestigious" and I was making such a good contact. This producer did all the casting; and when I met some of his actors, I knew I was in trouble before rehearsals began. The play was a stylized European comedy. The romantic lead he had engaged was a nice youth who would have been good playing a Brooklyn cop. The actor playing the butler was so busy flirting with the leading man that his attention was rarely on the script. The second lead was a wino. I visited him in his hotel room and found a great crock of cooking sherry there. With my promise that "I would not tell Dorothy Hammerstein" (a lady I have never even met, let alone shared secrets with), he let me pour it down the sink. This abrasive liquid was so strong that it severely damaged the plumbing in the hotel. That the old actor could still stand was a miracle to me when I saw what his tipple did to the tap water.

Since that nameless production I have permitted people to cast for me only on rare occasions. The drama critic of the New York Times sometimes criticizes producers for poor casting. He probably thinks he is being kind to the director. Actually, he is merely furthering the concept of "director as flunky."

THE ARTISTIC DIRECTOR

A new breed of producer is the regional theater "artistic director." Although those theaters are usually broke, they do have the virtue of being run by working directors. I will always remember with nostalgia the two plays I did for Gordon Davidson, when the Theatre Group was at U.C.L.A. I was running a theater myself at the time, and we had a mutual understanding of each other's needs. Unfortunately, with the move downtown to the Mark Taper Forum, some of the freedom and joy got mislaid. The Theatre Group's board of directors was joined by a number of people from Universal studios. I could never see the connection with the kind of product that studio turns out and the work of an art theater.

Soon after my production of *The Marriage of Mr. Mississippi* opened at the Forum, I ran into Gordon Davidson looking rather depressed. The reception had been mixed but not depressingly negative, so I said, "What's the matter with you?" He replied, "Ross Hunter hated it." I said, "Well, tell Mr. Hunter I didn't like

Midnight Lace!'' I do not know whether the message was ever relayed.

A few days later Gordon was looking cheerful and as he passed me he patted me on the arm and said, ''George Seaton loved it.'' As George Seaton wrote the script for *Coney Island*, a movie in which a director, played by George Montgomery, manacled the legs and arms of a performer, played by Betty Grable, to show her the virtue of stillness while singing, I at least knew that I had pleased a man of resource and imagination.

Recently I had a wonderful experience working with William Ross, artistic director of the Philadelphia Drama Guild that operates out of the historic Walnut Street Theater. He is such a fully rounded theater man himself that all his comments were wise and helpful.

This organization also has a man who is called the producer but is in fact a local dentist who raises the money for the company. One day after he had visited a rehearsal of *The Taming of the Shrew*, the play I was doing for them, he called me. His comments were among the most bizarre I have ever received from a producer. Here is part of our conversation:

Producer-Dentist: I listened to the record of *Taming of the Shrew* with Trevor Howard and he sounds quite different from Ron O'Neal.

Director: He *is* quite different. He's English and part of the tradition that goes back many years. Ron is a black American whose traditions and life-style are totally different.

Producer-Dentist: Couldn't you make him sound like Trevor Howard?

Director: No way. And even if there was, I wouldn't insult one good actor by trying to make him sound like another.

Producer-Dentist: Please do what you can.

Director: If you wanted someone sounding like Trevor Howard, why did you engage a star whose main claim to fame happens to be a movie called *Superfly*?

Producer-Dentist: We wanted to involve the black community in our activities. . . .

Ron O'Neal did amazingly well in the role, but he never sounded anything like Trevor Howard (see fig. 2).

The worst kind of producing director is the man who feels that he can ''fix up'' the work of his hireling. The only thing that can be said about these fellows is, Why didn't they undertake the job themselves in the first place?

In the past, the equivalent of an artistic director was often an actor-manager. I have worked in two theaters that were run by actors but strangely enough, the results were disastrous for the theaters. These men were simply unable to take an objective view of their producing and seemed to make most of their decisions from the point of view of satisfying their own actors' egos. In one instance, the artistic director had readily agreed to play the role I had cast him in. But once into rehearsal he made no secret of his resentment of another actor whom we had cast in a larger role. By his sulky and childish attitude the artistic director was sabotaging the very product that he was being handsomely paid to oversee.

I have found that the best producers are people who know either a great deal or absolutely nothing about the theater. Those in the latter category often come up with instinctive comments that are superbly objective and most valuable.

Despite the term ''academic freedom,'' one of the areas of the least directorial freedom is the university. Your production team is made up of colleagues who may or may not choose to be led by you. The cast has to come from a given pool of students, and as director, you are competing for everyone's time with a multitude of other activities. For junior faculty members, the situation is particularly tense because their whole future may depend on the production. I have seen graduate students, directing their thesis productions, literally age before my very eyes.

To end the discussion of producers on a positive note, let me relate a creative contribution that had wonderful results for me. The first producer who engaged me in the United States was Ethelyn Thrasher, who for some years ran the Playhouse-in-the-Park in Philadelphia. She already had a designer on her permanent staff. Charles Evans has now designed seventeen productions that I have directed, and ten others that I have produced. We have only had one disagreement. I should record that on that occasion, he was wrong!

**Second Phase
of Preparations**

We have now arrived at the second phase of our preparations. The decisions made at this point may very well make failure inevitable or, on the other end of the scale, they may make success a possibility. The former is easily achieved. The latter can only be worked for.

PLAYWRIGHTS

Let us assume that you have agreed to direct a new work. First, you have presumably insured that you can work with the author. I believe the playwright's function is by far the most important in the theater. This is so obvious to me that I would have omitted the statement had I not recently met a number of intelligent people who firmly believe that the actor is the principal creator of the theater. Good writers are rare and special creatures, and should be treated with great respect. Every actor and director should be made to write one play, so they can see how difficult it is. There have been a few examples of performers, like Nichols and May, who have created brilliant sketches, but most of the improvisational experiments that I have seen cannot compare with the work of a good dramatist. Writing and acting are totally different skills, and the duality of such talents as Molière and Shakespeare proves only that they were most unusual people.*

True, an actor can take a role and transform it into something

---

*Since writing this I have seen two very unusual living performers, John Kani and Winston Ntshona, who with playwright-director Athol Fugard created a masterpiece called *Sizwe Banzi Is Dead.*

that transcends even the author's wildest imaginings. If the basic plot line and characters are unsound, however, even a good actor will not be able to carry it off. There are far more good actors than there are good writers, hence actors frequently have to accept poor material to be able to continue in the business. Barely a week passes in New York City without some fine performer being hanged in the noose of a rotten script. A good director can help to cover the weakness of a play; but like the actor, he cannot make the unworkable work.

Playwrights are often difficult to work with. They have agonized over those lines in the solitude of their studies, and it is not surprising that they do not want to see anything changed or omitted. Almost all new plays are overwritten. Today's audiences are quick because they have become used to the fast cutting of film and television. Frequently the "feed" line gets the laugh because the audience has anticipated the joke.

Many inexperienced playwrights must be perusaded to *show* rather than *tell*. A former colleague, Bertram Joseph, speaks of good drama as "character in action"—a most apt phrase. Too many first plays are "character in explanation."

I have found that one of the best ways to help an author is to have him read his play aloud to me. Time and again, I have heard a playwright say, after a particularly awkward speech, "That's impossible, isn't it?" I also try to ask questions rather than just be critical. By answering those questions the writer can be helped to see the problems that he has created for the actor, the director, and the audience.

An author who is too acquiescent can be as big a problem as one who refuses to change a comma. I become terribly inhibited about questioning anything when I know that the author will immediately make a change, which will lack the conviction of the rest of the play. There are many examples of well-known playwrights who have given in to strong directors and permitted their plays to be ruined. There are just as many cases, however, where the author has stuck by his rights and destroyed the chances of the very play that he loved so much.

The only solution for this difficult, but immensely rewarding, relationship is for the director to gain the complete trust of the author. He must cherish this trust and not abuse it.

THE THEATER

A major consideration in this phase of the prerehearsal preparation is the nature of the theater in which the play will be performed. Until you know this, there is little point in talking to a designer. In fact, the designer you choose may depend on the stage you are using. Some designers are particularly good at making an off-Broadway flea pit look like a million dollars, while others can only function well with a large budget.

If you are going "out of town"—and most directors are spending more and more time "out of town"—ask for photographs of the theater and as many details as possible about its "special qualities" (no theater manager is going to use the word "limitations"). A production that really suits a house has much more of a chance to succeed than one that has been adapted to it. I am sure that one of the reasons *The Fantasticks* has met with such popularity at the Sullivan Street Theater is that it was brilliantly designed and staged for the particular environment of that theater. Similarly, I am sure that so many productions at the Mark Taper Forum in Los Angeles look uncomfortable largely because the material is invariably unsuited to that hybrid of a playhouse. It looks like a university lecture hall, and unless you are being lectured to, as in the case of *In the Matter of J. Robert Oppenheimer*, it is awfully hard to accept a conventional play there.

One of the many difficulties of directing off-Broadway is that the producers frequently do not know which theater they can get. This puts the director in the position of considering a show without knowing whether his work will be seen in a matchbox-sized proscenium or in a converted steambath. If fate gives you the right place, as it did to me when *The Curate's Play* was set in Saint George's Church, New York City, you are very fortunate (see fig. 3).

The University of Washington has three kinds of stages: proscenium, arena, and thrust. I could never convince my graduate students in directing that if they did not get the theater they wanted, they would then have to completely rethink the whole physical concept. You cannot just plunk a "thrust"-style production onto a proscenium stage.

The nature of the stage even affects casting. You might be

prepared to settle for a certain actor in an intimate house, whereas you know that in a larger theater he could not project past the first few rows.

DESIGNERS, SETTINGS, AND COSTUMES

The relationship between the director and the designer is almost as complex as that between the director and playwright. When a director finds a designer with whom he works well, he tends to hang onto him, as in the case of such superb partnerships as Tyrone Guthrie and Tanya Moiseiwitsch, and Hal Prince and Boris Aronson.

When a director goes out of town to an unfamiliar theater, he may only have a couple of days with the designer before he goes into rehearsals. Letters and phone calls are a chancy business. They only make it easier for both parties to misunderstand each other. When you arrive at a theater and the designer shows you a model of the set that makes it clear he has not even read the play properly, you have no option but to tell him exactly what to do. It is dreadful when this happens, because you are losing the possibility of a really creative contribution; but when there is no time, you have no alternative.

When I went to The North Carolina School of the Arts to do Pirandello's *Enrico IV*, I was presented, on my arrival, with a model of a set that was entirely scaffolding—something suitable for a medieval miracle play, but not for this sophisticated work. Had the designer read the script with even a minimum of care and intelligence, he would have seen that the text calls for construction of a scaffolding and the accouterments of "the Throne Room" *within* the environment of an Italian villa in the 1920s. The contrast between these fittings and the rest of the villa is as important as the contrast between the costumes of Enrico's "court" and the modern clothes of the visitors. I had no choice but to sit down with the designer and tell him exactly what had to be done.

A really good designer does not have to be told the obvious things that are needed for the set, such as the fact that Mark Antony needs to be raised for the Forum scene in *Julius Caesar*, or that Konstantin needs a stove in which to burn his manuscripts in the last act of *The Seagull*. Working with a true artist, like Charles

Evans, all I had to do was discuss the play and the values that I hoped to bring out. If you are working with a designer you do not know, the best mutual vocabulary is that of familiar artists. If you tell a designer that you want the play to look as if Rembrandt had painted it, he will probably know what you mean.

When I worked at the Old Globe in San Diego, I had never previously met the designer, Peggy Kellner. I showed her a small reproduction of a sixteenth-century fresco from Lombardy, which inspired her to create a whole world for *All's Well That Ends Well*. Every time I read the piece I became increasingly alarmed at the improbabilities of the plot. We are asked to believe that a woman changes places with another in the bed of the man she loves, who is so blissfully unaware of the fact that he goes ahead and impregnates her. We must gather from this amazing incident (it happens in *Measure for Measure* as well) that at least two of Shakespeare's heroes were very unobservant. In thinking about the play and its origins (it was one of Boccaccio's tales), I concluded that the only way to do it was to present it as a yarn. The fresco had the right feeling for the storybook illusion I wanted to create. Peggy went one further and painted a beautiful drop curtain, which looked like the frontispiece for a book of Renaissance tales. The design reproduced in fugure 4 is for the Duke of Florence. I asked her for the Renaissance Italian equivalent of General Patton. This sketch is what she came up with.

Some of the angriest disagreements I have had in the theater have been with designers. It has invariably been because the finished work bore no resemblance to the original sketches. I have been accused of suffocating designers by imposing my own ideas on them. This has usually happened when I was pressured for time and just had to have something on paper with which to start work. I cannot deal with designers who feel that their artistic creation is more important than the needs of the production as a whole. If the audience can remember nothing of the evening but the scenery, then their outing has been a failure. A set can be a thing of great beauty, yet still evoke something dirty and sordid like David Jenkins' *Changing Room*; or make the ultimate comment on modern New York City like Boris Aronson's sensational steel structure for *Company*; or provide the anchor for a whole production concept like Stephen Hendrickson's plastic set for my *A Midsum-*

Stage setting by Charles Evans for *Philadelphia, Here I Come,* Playhouse
Theatre Company, Vancouver, B.C., 1968

Tammy Grimes and Ron O'Neal in *The Taming of the Shrew,* produced by
Bill Ross for the Philadelphia Drama Guild at the Walnut Street Theater, 1974

Stage structure designed by Peter Wexler for *The Curate's Play,* produced in
Saint George's Church, New York City, in 1961. Sketch copyright by
Peter Wexler, 1961

mer Night's Dream in Los Angeles. In other words, a designer need not swallow his creativity in serving the needs of everyone else.

If your costume and set designer are different people, it is essential that they work closely together. I will never forget Alec Guinness' London *Hamlet* in which the Switzers had one black leg to their tights. Standing in front of a black drape they looked as if they had all lost the same leg in battle.

I have noticed that good designers usually come to rehearsals from time to time, and they will sometimes suggest changes in design details to facilitate what is being done by the actors. Whether they visit you or not, it is essential that they know of any unusual things that you plan. If you have someone doing a cartwheel in a farthingale (I have seen more unlikely things at Stratford, Connecticut), the designer must have this information in order to adapt the costume accordingly. Similarly, if a piece of furniture is to be given particularly rough usage, it must be constructed especially for the stage business.

Although I have spoken only of set and costume designers, the same principles apply to people who design the lights. Unless they are involved as early as possible, they cannot be expected to produce illumination and effects that will suit the whole production. The main problem I have encountered with these people is a tendency to concentrate too much on effect and not enough on illumination. It is my opinion that unless you have a superb artist like Tharon Musser or Judy Rasmuson, of the Long Wharf, it is best for the set and lighting designers to be the same person. You are certainly more likely to end up with something that resembles the original sketch.

When I first went to the Crest Theatre in Toronto, the theater had a brilliant scene painter named Murray Laufer, who has subsequently become one of Canada's best scene designers. He told me how frustrating it was that the lighting always changed or even obliterated his painting. I found out fairly soon what the lighting designer's problem was: he was color blind!

INCIDENTAL MUSIC AND COMPOSERS

Music for plays is either ''incidental'' or ''source.'' Incidental music underscores action, introduces a scene, or fills in a set change. Source music has an actual source on stage, such as a bugle or a record player.

If you are going to use incidental music for the production, you will probably have to make a tape from existing recordings. This practice is illegal but frequent. You may be fortunate enough to have a producer who will agree to an original score that is specially recorded or even played live. I feel lucky to have worked with such composers as Arnold Black (no relation), Rupert Black (my nephew), Lee Michaels, and Conrad Susa, who have created tapes that contributed immeasurably to plays that I have directed. They suggested places for music cues, and so did I. These collaborations produced some first-rate theater music.

I will always remember one time when Conrad Susa was sitting in on a rehearsal of *All's Well That Ends Well*. During a break after running a scene, he came up to me and said: "You know, that is being acted in a totally different manner than you had described. If you have changed your mind, then I must rethink the music in this scene." I ran the scene again and saw exactly what he meant. I had become carried away by what was happening between the actors, and we had indeed strayed from the essentials. Maestro Susa did not have to alter his composition.

The reason there is so little music used for plays in New York City is that the cost is prohibitive. Luckily there was no musicians' union around when Lully, Grieg, and Delius were writing for the theater.

A word of advice to any director who is using recorded music and has access to New York City. If you ever get stuck for an idea or need help in your selection, go to Music Masters on West Forty-third Street and ask for Willy Lerner. If you tell him what you want the music to do, he will invariably come up with the perfect choice.

PUBLICITY AND PROGRAM NOTES

Most producers feel that publicity and posters are their prerogative. I certainly did. A good press agent will always get together with the director. If the publicity is misleading, the production can be hurt.

When the Royal Shakespeare Company appeared in Los Angeles, it seemed that the publicity was centered on the nude

Helen of Troy in Marlowe's *Doctor Faustus*. From the laugh that greeted the famous line, "Is this the *face* that launched a thousand ships?" spoken by Faustus when she finally reached him after an interminable stage cross, it was apparent that many of the audience were not there primarily because of their great interest in Elizabethan drama.

Regional theaters usually ask for a program piece from the director. I used to think that the finished work on stage was the best program piece, but I have been won around to the opposite point of view. An audience rarely needs guidance, but these director's notes seem to help the critics. In some places they will paraphrase great chunks of the program in their review. So do not write anything you do not want to see on newsprint. In more sophisticated communities you may be taken to task for not doing what you claimed to be aiming for in your program notes. If the play is an historical one, some notes on the background are valuable. I also think that for complicated plots, as in Jacobean tragedies, it is a good idea to spell out the family relationships in the list of characters.

I believe anything that will make the experience more enjoyable for the audience is worth putting in the program. I also believe that some of the program notes one sees are so pretentious that one is put off the production even before the curtain goes up.

In reviewing the David Rabe play, *The Orphan*, most of the New York critics commented on the elaborate program notes, not only by the author but by producer Joseph Papp as well. The general feeling was that a play needing that much explanation was obviously in trouble even before the curtain went up.

Casting

Most producers tend to leave the design work pretty much to the director and his relevant cohorts, provided that they are not exceeding their budget. Casting is another matter. I find this to be the area in which everyone and his mother wants to help.

Directors usually start their casting by going out after specific actors. This is the bane of the unemployed actor's life. If a director has worked well with a performer, however, then he obviously wants to repeat the good experience. I am always making mental notes of actors whose work I have enjoyed. When the right opportunity occurs, I automatically put a call out for them. If nobody you know of is available for each role, then you start looking for people who are new to you.

In working with other people on casting, I have found it a good idea to figure out an "ideal" list of actors. If you tell the casting director, or the university acting teacher, that you see Dick Cavett as Iago, everyone knows it is out of the question, but they will know how you see the role. In professional theater, availability and money are large considerations. The first is self-explanatory. The second is frequently a nightmare. You want someone for a role, but the producer will not pay their price. Sometimes I have been told that someone is unavailable when, in fact, the producer was simply waiting for me to come up with a cheaper actor. Agents, especially in Los Angeles, will often do anything to pre-

22

vent you from getting a client because the theater is not as profitable for them as film or television. They would much sooner have their client doing a feminine hygiene commercial than playing Ophelia at some Shakespeare festival.

There are some agents who are smart enough to realize that their clients will eventually make them much richer from exposure in good roles in the theater. Alas, these far-sighted folk seem to be a dying breed, or like the Heifetz of theater agents, my own much-missed Jane Dreyfuss, they marry a nice person and leave the business.

ACTORS EQUITY ASSOCIATION

Another frequent problem is the union question. A management may not want to pay to have parts played by people who are in Actors Equity Association when they can use students or amateurs in the roles. It has always seemed absurd to me that a union can on one hand demand that people join it in order to work professionally, and then at the same time permit other people to appear on stage for nothing. And I am not speaking only of bit parts or walk-ons. I cannot entirely blame producers for taking advantage of these concessions.

Like everything else, casting deliberations will usually result in a compromise. The best argument I can give for the employment of the professional is a production I did of *Lock Up Your Daughters* for the Pasadena Playhouse. None of the students who auditioned was ready to play the character roles with which that show abounds. The producer agreed to let me have four extra Equity people. The result was the most successful show in that theater for thirty years. Even though the Playhouse was virtually bankrupt, the producer made a decision that paid off. The performances in tiny character parts by people like Bill Christopher and Eric Brotherson were irreplaceable contributions.(See fig. 9.)

BALANCE IN CASTING

I am convinced that the essence of casting is balance. If your Hamlet is a good actor but not an overwhelming personality, you will not help him by engaging an overpowering Horatio. I do not mean that you should get poor supporting actors just to make your lead look better, but simply that you should look for a Horatio who will complement him.

When actors show me reviews that refer to their ''scene-stealing cameos,'' I am immediately put off. I am interested in people who contribute to a scene, not people who throw it out of balance. A good actor will clearly reveal his talent without doing it at the expense of everyone else. I will never forget Alec Guinness with the Old Vic just after the war, playing Abel Drugger in *The Alchemist*, or Morris Carnovsky as Dr. Caius in *The Merry Wives of Windsor* at Stratford, Connecticut—brilliant performances in minor roles that never overstepped the needs of the productions as a whole. I am sure everyone has seen the kind of work I am speaking of, just as they have seen some selfish ham overdo the lesser moments and ruin the whole balance of a play.

If a production has one or two people who, as it were, come with the deal, it can often be very hard to cast the other parts. Say the play is *Romeo and Juliet*, and Juliet is a fine actress but clearly too old for the role; then you have the problem of finding a Romeo who will not make the play look like *Tea and Sympathy*.

"NAMES"

Another problem can be the whole question of ''names.'' Personally, I doubt that there are more than a handful of stars who really sell tickets in the theater. I believe it is a combination of the play and the actor, in that order, that attracts the public. A perfect example was Mary Martin in *The Sound of Music*, a big hit followed by Mary Martin in *Jenny*, which flopped. If the production is simply a vehicle for a star, as is often the case in stock packages, then it had better be a play that is suitable. It can be horrendous for everyone when a star is trying to make an impact in a role that is clearly not designed as the center of focus.

AUDITIONS

There are many views on auditions. The worst manifestation of these are the Equity ''open'' calls, which I find totally degrading for the actor and impossible for the director. I personally can only look properly at about twenty people in one day. After that, it is simply a matter of the law of diminishing returns.

I have found that the best method of conducting an "open" audition is to ask actors to prepare something of their own choosing. If I were doing a Christopher Fry play, I would ask for a piece from a modern play in verse and give the actors the widest possible choice for the first meeting. I think a director can learn a great deal about an actor's self-image from the kind of material he picks. Actors who see themselves realistically are much easier to work with than those who have an illusion about the way they appear to the world.

The fewer people who are with you at the first audition the better. It is a ghastly experience for the actor at best. If he has to come in, usually after a long wait, and be presented to a whole string of associate producers, friends of the choreographer, and coffee-swilling secretaries, he will only be more uncomfortable.

I think it is only fair to talk with the artist for a little before the ordeal, to break the ice. At the first meeting I find this time frequently much more valuable than the actual audition. I always like to know what role they are interested in, even at this stage. If the phone rings during an audition (why does it always?), stop the actor and let him start again in his own time. Many people believe in having the auditioning actor read from the script at their first meeting. I am very much against it. All I get from this is the knowledge of how good they may be at sight reading, and how good they are at controlling a shaking hand. The time to have the actors read from the script is when you have called them back and have an idea of which part they might be suitable for.

FITTING THE ACTOR TO THE PART

I want to emphasize the word "suitable" in the preceding paragraph because I think suitability is the key. I do not subscribe to the belief that an actor should be able to play anything. If a person does not have something in his own personality that would work for the part, I see no point in asking him to play it. The most interesting type of casting occurs when a director senses a quality in an actor that has not previously been brought out. When I am down to the stage of reading for specific roles, an actor will sometimes give me a completely new idea of how a part can be played. When I was doing Next Time I'll Sing to You for Gordon Davidson in Los Angeles, I had mixed ideas as to how the Hermit should be played. Robert Casper came in to see me and to explain why he should play the role of Rudge. As he talked I realized I had found the definitive Hermit! (See fig. 5.)

In a repertory company you often have to miscast. This can be interesting and rewarding for the actors and a challenge to the director, but it is usually frustrating for the audience. In a single play, I am not interested in unnecessary experimentation; there are enough risks involved already. If you want to assume the responsibility of making key decisions, the least you can do for your producers and their backers is not jeopardize their investment to satisfy the ego of an actor.

In the educational situation, the aim is only for the good of the student. Therefore, you should always be prepared to jeopardize the end result to provide individuals with a valuable experience. Incidentally, another important consideration in educational theater is the student's willingness to play the role you assign. Students tend to be deplorably choosy about what they will or will not play. The poor professional can rarely afford to be so particular.

When I am down to my final choices, I like to have people in together. It is good to see how Caesar looks and sounds with Cleopatra. If some roles have been precast, I still ask those performers in to see them with the actors I am considering. By the final auditions, I do not mind having other people present. The final cast is going to have to perform in public anyway, and if they go to pieces before extra people, you might as well find out then. Also, I think that producers should be in on the final decisions. The author, of course, has a contractual right to give or withhold approval.

I find making decisions regarding actors to be very difficult; but as the years go by, I am better able to distinguish between an actor's façade and an actor's self. If there are any rules for picking performers, I am afraid I do not know them. I think it just has to be an instinct, and different directors are attracted by different actors. I remember one time I was doing *Critic's Choice* in stock, and an agent suggested George Segal for the part of the young director. The artistic director of the theater happened to be there and assured me that I would not be interested. But from the moment George came into the office, I was amused and intrigued by him.

He had read the play and in reading for me, he was immediately able to translate his own delightful personality into the scene that he was reading. Yet it was not a finished performance like a radio reading, but the beginnings of one of the funniest characterizations I have ever seen on the stage. He has, of course, subsequently become a big movie star. Thank heaven Hollywood has finally given up trying to make him into a new John Garfield and is letting him play comedy on the screen.

The thing I look for in a reading is an indication that the actor can "imagine" and not just "read." If an actor can create a life for the lines and situation of the play, he is likely to reveal this ability fairly quickly by his eyes. Even if the person he is reading with is the assistant stage manager, an actor will still begin to react. Too many actors try to play on their own lines and have no life going on for their character.

I once did a play with Dana Elcar, who was so alive to everything that was happening around him that I would swear he could even incorporate a passing police siren into his acting consciousness. He would "pick up" on everything that another actor did and help everyone in the scene with him to give more. An actor friend of mine once worked with a selfish actress in a role for which he grew a mustache during rehearsals. At the closing night party, the actress came up to him and said, "Why, Bob, you've grown a mustache." She had obviously paid absolutely no attention to him in the play.

When you are casting a play and think that your own personal prejudices and biases are influencing your choice, you must pay particular attention to the opinions of the other people. If you are overly impressed by an ingénue, it may not be her acting ability that makes you react so positively. Listen to the opinions of others, but in the end you must make up your own mind and be prepared to ignore everyone else's advice. You may not win a popularity contest with your employers, but you stand a sporting chance of coming up with a good show.

The Final Stage of
Prerehearsal Preparation

The final stage of prerehearsal preparation is a solitary time, but for the director a good time. I know a lot of people who go away to be alone with their script and their floor plans. After going through all the activities that I have described, it is always a relief to get back to the play itself.

REREADING THE PLAY

I like to reread the play, visualizing the actors we have employed as the characters and starting to think of the physical shape that the staging will take. The cast is rarely the perfect one, and there usually has to be some rethinking now to make the play work in terms of the actual people you have.

I find that most good plays have scenes that divide into subscenes. In each of these something is revealed, something happens, or a question is established for the audience—or maybe a combination of all three. The director cannot go into rehearsal until he knows not only the overall aim of the play but the way in which each act, scene, and subscene contributes to it.

After reading each section of the action, you must know exactly what is happening and why. The director even at this stage must consider each scene from the point of view of the audience. If the purpose of a subscene preceding an emotional denouement is to relax the audience so that the upcoming shock will be greater, then you must think of ways to achieve this.

If the play concerns a milieu with which you are familiar, your research will be minimal. If you are doing a play by Shakespeare, and you do not happen to be a scholar, then you will have a great deal of work to do. The third time I directed *Romeo and Juliet* I really felt that I knew the text well. On this occasion I worked with Bertram Joseph on the play and I was horrified to find out how much I had missed.

There is a basic difference between the function of a scholar and that of a director. The scholar may be concerned with the pursuit of knowledge, through research and insight, for its own sake. As a director you are concerned with the way in which you can apply the scholar's information to your own work and make the text more meaningful to your actors. It is not enough to explain the divine right of kings to a high school student playing King Lear. You must show how that position makes certain actions inevitable and how that position is regarded by the other characters. An actor cannot be an imposing monarch in the first act of *King Lear* unless the other actors on the stage are acknowledging his majesty and are aware of the way in which it affects their behavior and attitudes.

CUTTING THE PLAY

This is the stage at which you must do any editing that may be necessary—assuming, of course, that the playwright is not around! In Shakespeare's plays, cuts are made today for a number of reasons, some of them quite bizarre. When I was in the Old Vic Company, Her Majesty Queen Elizabeth II was to attend the opening night of *Henry VIII*. After the dress rehearsal the director, Tyrone Guthrie, informed us that he had been advised that the show was running ten minutes over the time that Her Royal Highness liked to remain in the theater. For that reason he had to crop ten minutes out of the playing time. I have often wondered what would happen if this royal personage decided to honor an opening of *Parsifal* at Bayreuth.

The first things that I cut in Shakespeare are the jokes that mean nothing to a contemporary audience. This may sound rather arrogant, but if I have to spend a considerable amount of time researching the point of a joke, I assume that most of the audience will not find the jest amusing. In other words, my definition of an obscure joke is one that I do not get. I also try to cut repetitions. I really do not think it is necessary today for Friar Lawrence to recap the whole of *Romeo and Juliet* in the final moments of the play. When one tries to visualize the Elizabethan playhouse, one can easily see why it was necessary to keep reiterating the plot line. The noise and other distractions must have been incredible. One of the problems in cutting the bard is that some of the most beautiful passages are the easiest to cut. The famous "arias" always reveal character, but they do not always advance the action.

PLANNING

There are different views on prerehearsal blocking. I know directors who plan every move ahead of time with chessmen in the model. I know others who block on their feet at rehearsal with the actors. The amount that I do depends entirely on the play. If you have one of those huge scenes at the end of an old-fashioned musical where everyone is getting together, then you have to figure it out precisely. Otherwise that awful moment at rehearsal will occur when a character has an aside to someone, and that someone is way over on the other side of the stage. If you are doing a murder mystery, or a French farce, you will have to preplan everything because these plays are constructed like jigsaw puzzles.

At the risk of generalizing, I would say that you should always plan exits, entrances, key moves, and important business; but some of the blocking can evolve in rehearsals. The amount of such planning must also depend on the people you are going to work with. If you are directing students or amateurs, you will probably have to give them every move, and you should prepare for that eventuality. If the set design is a good one, and the positions of furniture, entrances, and props are correct, planning of blocking and subsequent staging is not difficult. If the layout of the set is poor, you are in for a rehearsal nightmare.

The creation of suitable floor plans is a subject for a book in itself, but there are certain important points that should be considered. The first is suitability for the play and its action. If you have an interior that must contain a number of people, then you cannot have your stage cluttered with unnecessary furniture. Settings for big rooms are obviously easier to stage in than small ones; but if the set is, let us say, the tenement in *A Taste of Honey*, you have to give the audience an impression of clutter. This means using your small space in a precise manner. An actor a couple of feet in the wrong position can mask something important in a small set.

The key sections of the set must be clearly visible. If you want a love scene played in a recumbent position, then the bed must be placed where everyone in the audience can see it, well within the sight lines (the area of the stage visible to all the seats in the audience). Most theaters have many seats from which the whole stage cannot be seen. Two of the most highly praised productions at Britain's National Theatre have been *The National Health* and *The Misanthrope*. I saw both from the side of the orchestra and paid the top price. "Saw" is not the right word. Key scenes of both plays were obstructed either by actors badly placed or overlarge furniture placed downstage. Either the directors sat only in the center of the theater or they just did not care. On a stage such as that at the Old Vic, which is the width of the house, there is no excuse for cheating the audience.*

Good floor plans give you space between doors and windows as well as between the important pieces of furniture. In domestic interiors it can be quite hard to devise interesting movement, so the more you can separate important furniture and the various entrances the more opportunities you have for movement.

The best way to illustrate the difference between good and adequate is to show a floor plan that gave me problems alongside the layout that I would have liked. The play, *The House of Blue Leaves*, is a joy to direct. I did it for the graduating class of 1973 at the Juilliard and found them to be a wonderfully gifted group. Floor plan 1 is the plan I had originally. I showed it to my good friend J. B. Keene, who is a very fine designer. As a means of illustrating the difference between awkward design and skillful, Jaye drew the second floor plan for me. Many of the advantages are obvious, but let me point out a few of the improvements.

The first plan is symmetrical. Unless one is trying to make a

---

*The current Broadway hit *Same Time Next Year* is playing at the Brooks Atkinson Theater, which has poor sight lines from the seats at the side of the orchestra. Although the play concerns marital infidelity, the bed is stage right. For $12.00 all I saw when the characters were abed was their feet.

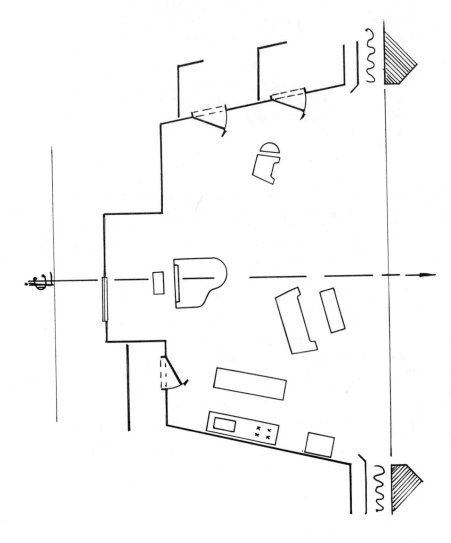

Floor plan 1 for *The House of Blue Leaves*

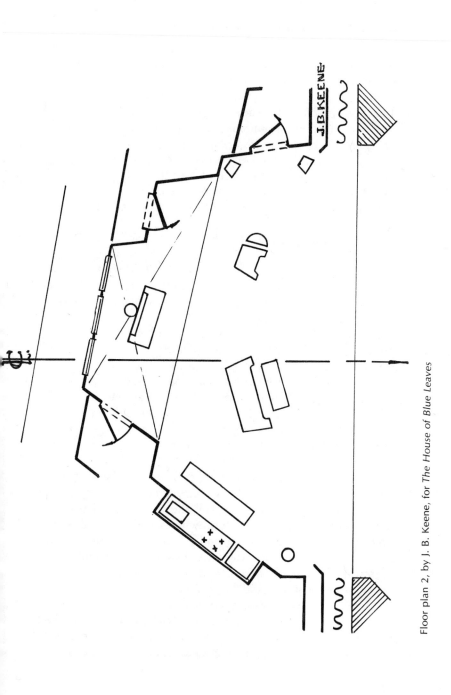

Floor plan 2, by J. B. Keene, for *The House of Blue Leaves*

specific point by this, such layouts are to be avoided. They look boring and tend to lead one into dull groupings. On stage right Jaye has created an alcove for the kitchen equipment, giving me a clear passage behind the counter. The level in the large upstage alcove again makes for variety, but it also puts the upstage left door, which is the main entrance, into a prominent position. In the first plan this entrance is badly placed. The larger window not only makes better architectural sense, but in this play three nuns have to come through it. In the second plan this entrance is greatly facilitated. The comparison of these two drawings mainly shows the great difference made by comparatively small variations in design.

In opera and musicals, the plotting of the action in the sung scenes is entirely contingent on the music. If the tenor only has four bars to leave his supper and get the knife from the cabinet, then the table and said cabinet must be exactly the right distance for him to do it to the music. There is a reason for little variation in opera staging from house to house.

Jan Rubes, the Canadian basso, told me an interesting story about *The Marriage of Figaro* at Stratford, Ontario. It was to be staged by a comparative newcomer to opera, Jean Gascon. All the singers agreed beforehand to forget the traditional things they were accustomed to in that opera. By the end of the third week, however, Gascon had arrived at an overall production in which they were back to much of their usual moves and business simply because, as Rubes put it, "There are certain things in *Figaro* that you can only do one way!"

The length of rehearsal has a lot to do with your planning. If you have a month or more, you know that you can experiment; but if you are doing stock, which usually allows only one week, you have to come to the first rehearsal with everything minutely figured out. The first play I did under these conditions was *The Pleasure of His Company* with the delightful Murray Matheson. I found that show a nightmare to work out, because I kept losing the positions of the glasses and the state of the drinks. It seemed that on every line someone was referring to the need for a "fill-up." I made the mistake in my initial planning of following the published script of the Broadway production, only to find that the notations were contradictory. At the first rehearsal I only mislaid a couple of

Costume design by Peggy Kellner for the Duke of Florence in *All's Well That Ends Well,* Old Globe Theater, San Diego, 1967

Robert Casper as The Hermit in *Next Time I'll Sing to You,* U.C.L.A. Theatre Group, 1966

Walter Pidgeon in the title role of *Lord Pengo,* 1963 stock tour

Hutchinson Shandro, John Juliani, Neil Dainard (left to right, rear), and Brenda Ellis (foreground) in *The Knack*, Playhouse Theatre Company, Vancouver, B.C., 1965

Barbara Babcock, Monty Landis, James B. Douglas, Antoinette Bower, Bill Wintersole, Ronald Long, and Patrick Horgan in the U.C.L.A. Theatre Group production of *Poor Bitos*, 1967

Peter Church, Holly Harris, and Murray Matheson in the Pasadena Playhouse production of *Lock Up Your Daughters,* 1968

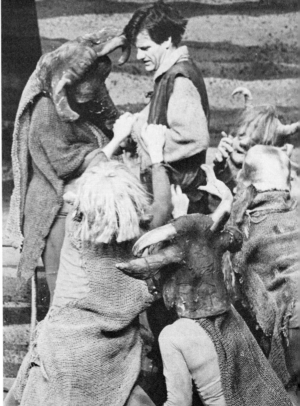

Neil Dainard as *Peer Gynt,* Playhouse Theatre Company, Vancouver, B.C., 1967

glasses, but it was really amazing how so small an item could be such a big problem.

The only comprehensive answer to the question of how much preparation a director should do is to say that you should not go into rehearsal until you feel you can answer any question about the play that is asked. The fun of rehearsals is the other things you discover, and the wonderful things that your actors will show you.

The First
Day of Rehearsal

Somebody once told me that he felt the director's primary function on the first day of rehearsal was to get the day over with as quickly as possible. It certainly is a time that can strike terror into the hearts of even the most experienced actors (and directors), comparable only to the horror of the first night. One of the advantages of the repertory company set-up is that most of the people know each other already.

ELECTING A DEPUTY

There are usually various business things that have to be done, information that the stage manager will need to give. I always believe in starting out with all these things. The laughter that usually accompanies the reading of the Actors Equity piece on electing a deputy is a good means of relaxing people in itself. If the company is operating on a ''stock'' contract, the director is covered by the same union as the actor and is entitled to join in the election of the deputy (or shop steward). I am in four unions—Equity, American Guild of Musical Artists (for opera), Directors Guild of America (film and television), and the Society of Stage Directors and Choreographers—but in many productions that I have done, I have not been covered by any of them. As the director is, in many ways, part of ''management,'' there is not much the actor's union can do to protect him from himself. Equity has yet to prepare a contract form for the director; we are signed on an actor's contract even though much of the wording and rules is inapplicable to us. Two things Equity can do for a director are to set certain minimums for fees and provide the bond. This bond is a sum of money that management is supposed to deposit with Equity to cover salaries for one or two weeks. The amount varies according to the producer's reputation for reliability. These bonds are not always posted, and the actors do still get stuck sometimes with useless checks and even have to pay their own fares home. As the director gets paid no later than opening night, he is less likely to get caught.

INTRODUCTORY REMARKS

I once attended the first rehearsal of a production at Stratford, Connecticut, at which the director talked from 11:00 A.M. until nearly 4:00 in the afternoon. By the time the reading got under way, everyone was half asleep. I believe that a few introductory remarks by the director are appropriate. Even a word of welcome from the producers can be a pleasant thing. When I was running the Vancouver Playhouse, I always used to introduce the guest director to the company myself. I have always appreciated it when people have done this for me. You should always show the actors the costume designs and the model of the set so that they can better imagine the world that the play will eventually inhabit. It is also a good way of introducing the designers and involving them with the actors.

THE FIRST READINGS

If the cast is small, it is always easier to have everyone sit around a table. When the cast is large, you are stuck with a rather impersonal semicircle. I encourage the actors to act and characterize as much or as little as they feel like doing at the first reading. I do not interrupt until a scene break, unless someone asks me a question about the meaning of something or a pronunciation problem comes up. If the names are unusual, I give their pronunciations before the reading. I like actors who have scenes together to sit together. Performers who use the reading properly will start to make contact within the context of the scenes; but since some good actors simply cannot read well, I do not make a big point of this.

During the first reading, some actors will show clear indications of work they have already done. If they are obviously off in the wrong direction, you should point this out immediately. You must be careful, however, not to inhibit them when trying to rechannel their imaginations. I think any director prefers an actor who comes to rehearsal full of ideas than one who waits to be guided all the way.

The number of read-throughs depends on many things, primarily the length of the rehearsal period. In stock there is rarely time for any readings at all. If I have three weeks to rehearse, I like two readings, the first one going straight through the play, and then a second during which I like to stop a lot and encourage the actors to do the same thing. Some plays, Chekhov's in particular, benefit from a lengthy exploration before the actors get on their feet. Others of a more physical nature, like farces, can only be rehearsed with the moves.

THE DIRECTOR'S AUTHORITY

I believe that success in gaining the trust and confidence of actors depends greatly on the director's ability to provide each actor with the kind of direction that he personally needs. Some actors like to be pushed, even bullied, while others are best left alone in the early stages of rehearsal. In this respect it is an enormous advantage to be working with actors you know.

In many situations you find that there will be one or two people in the cast who consider themselves "stars" of the group. The more bucolic the location of the theater, the more likely this is to occur. Oddly enough, the real "stars" that I have worked with are usually the least inclined to elicit special treatment, although there are exceptions. If a selfish attitude is clearly interfering with the rehearsals, then the director must make it quite clear to the offending performer that if the whole production is good, then he or she is more likely to score on opening night. The important thing is the show and not the ego of an individual actor.

The same thing can be said for the director. If he has to continually force his authority down everyone's throat, he will not get the best contribution from the whole cast. I have seen directors reject first-rate suggestions simply because they clearly did not have the confidence in themselves to admit that other people could think of things they had not. Directors like that are simply putting their vanity before the production. On the other hand, a rehearsal is not just a free-for-all. It is the director's job to see that everything that happens in rehearsal is of value. When a discussion, even at the first reading, passes the point of usefulness, the director must end it.

Until I know actors, and they know each other, I make my directions to them alone. I feel that what I have to say is between us. Even after there is perfect rapport among everyone, I think there are certain kinds of notes, personal things, that are only the business of the director and the individual actor. I have a friend who is a very good director, popular with actors, who gives every note at the top of his voice. He maintains that everything he says should affect everybody and he wants all to hear. It is simply a question of each director finding the way that works for him. I think my friend's method is the correct one for educational theater, where the prime purpose is the learning experience. Students can learn from notes given to others as well as to themselves.

The important thing on the first day is for the director to establish an atmosphere in which people can start to work.

The Stage Manager and His Function

As I have done quite a bit of stage managing myself, I hold strong views on the position. In rehearsal the stage manager is responsible for making the director's life as uncomplicated as possible. He cannot work to a rule book, and should be prepared to do anything that will make the rehearsals go more smoothly. He should always anticipate the needs of the director and the actors. His rehearsal role is something between that of a top sergeant and a major domo. His specific responsibilities are manifold.

He coordinates all the activities of the creative people. He arranges the rehearsal calls, fittings, and press interviews. He is responsible for the discipline of rehearsals and performances.

He and his assistants make notes of all the moves and stage business during rehearsals, and prepare the prop list, adding to it on a day-to-day basis. If it becomes obvious that a detail of a scene will not work in the set or costume design, he must be the liaison between the director and the designer—a job that requires great diplomacy. Prompting at rehearsals is an art in itself, a mixture of tact and theatrical instinct.

During rehearsals, he can frequently act as an intermediary between people who are misunderstanding one another. Although he works *with* the director, he is working *for* the producer, and he may on occasion have to go to the producer to tell him that the director is not achieving the results that he should in the time he has expended.

As the production moves into the theater, he becomes the backstage overlord. During the technical rehearsals, he starts calling the cues (lighting, sound, scene changes) for the show. Once the play has opened, he takes over the responsibility for the production. His presence at the rehearsals enables him to be in constant touch with the director's intentions. A knowledge of these is essential if he is to maintain the concept once the run is underway. As he is also responsible for rehearsing understudies and replacements, he must be able to function *in loco parentis* for the director.

There are two main reasons why good stage managers are in short supply. The first is that the position is one of the best stepping stones to becoming a producer or director, so the turnover is fast. The second is that not many people can and will do so many things. Take the matter of discipline. With a musical there are always a lot of people around, and the noise in a large, echoing rehearsal room is deafening. If a stage manager simply screams at people to ''shut up,'' he is merely adding to the noise. If he finds a place outside where people can wait until they are needed, he makes life easier for everyone. If his director is disorganized, the stage manager can compensate by providing the order that is lacking. He must anticipate everything.

I remember the first time I worked with Dorothy Fowler in Philadelphia. When I arrived, a table for me and chairs for the actors were all set up, and she even had a box of sharpened pencils in anticipation of the fact that actors often forget to bring anything to write with.

When I was a stage manager, and was working with a weak director, the temptation to make unsolicited suggestions was sometimes overwhelming. It has to be resisted, however. In Vancouver I had the services of the inestimable Ronald Pollock, now dean of drama at the North Carolina School of Arts. Once we had established the fact that I welcomed his comments *after* rehearsals, I had a continual fund of helpful and creative suggestions.

The problem with many stage managers, in this country, is that they make it quite clear they consider themselves superior to the job. They also shy away from taking any responsibility that they can avoid. These people forget that their primary purpose is to do anything that will make rehearsals smoother, and the subsequent show a better one. Interestingly, the stage managers I have known who have functioned effectively are the very ones who have gone on to other positions.

I am convinced that stage managing is excellent preparation for becoming a director. By being at the center of everything, the stage manager gets the best overall view of the production. I found I learned even more about directing from stage managing for incompetent directors than I did from the good people I worked with.

When a stage manager is ineffective, sometimes it is because the director does not know how to use him properly. If at the first rehearsal you go to the stage manager and tell him that you are ready to begin, rather than yourself yelling, "Quiet, please!" then you are immediately letting him know that you will work through him. When you tell an actor that he can come in late the next day, how can the stage manager keep track of everyone and demand punctuality? A director who arrives late for every rehearsal (my wife once worked for a young director in the Northwest who was up to an hour late on most days) makes it impossible for the stage manager to run an effective rehearsal. The more you involve your stage manager with the production and your own work on it, the more likely he is to contribute at every level.

In referring to stage managers, I find that I have consistently used the masculine gender. This is simply a convenience. In fact, I have found that women tend to make better stage managers than men. I do not pretend to know the reason, but it may have to do with the fact that they are less discontented with the position than their male counterparts. Although "Gay Liberation" probably originated in the theater, "Women's Lib" has yet to create total equality of opportunity anywhere but on the stage.

The Rehearsal Period

In the preceding chapters I have spoken of possible time variations in the rehearsal period. As a director you may be involved in rehearsals that span two months at one extreme and the stock schedule of one week at the other. When I was free-lancing exclusively, I found that the continual adjustments I had to make were very difficult. After doing a summer of package tours with only eight days before opening, I would suddenly find myself in the fall with four weeks to rehearse. I then had to guard constantly against a tendency to go too quickly.

TIME

In my work I have found that my life is largely governed by time. I am particularly conscious of the length of a minute, having worked for the BBC in both live radio and television. Although it is impossible to gauge exactly how long you will need to work on a scene, you have to have some idea of how much you should be able to do in a given time span.

Take a hypothetical situation: It is the dress rehearsal of *Fiddler on the Roof*. The time is 11:00 P.M. You have the full orchestra for the last time prior to opening. In an hour the musicians will leave and the crew will go on double time. You have to decide which things to spend time on and which things to leave until later. The choice should be made on the basis of which adjustments require the full company, stage, and musicians. If it is a problem involving only a few people, like the scenes in Tevya's house, you can do it in the rehearsal room the next day.

Another example might well be the wedding reception, which is the first act finale. Everybody in the show is involved in this, and the way most musical theaters are run, it is likely that the cast is working with the scenic elements and the props for the first time. This scene requires a perfect coordination of acting, singing, dancing, and orchestra accompaniment. Therefore, *now* is the last chance that you, the choreographer, and the conductor have to get it right.

This example is one extreme, but even in the comparative leisure of a college campus, an evening rehearsal that has not been used well is an evening rehearsal that you will regret by the opening. One of the most frustrating things in academic theater is the way students are so extravagant with that precious commodity: time.

STAGING

Let us assume that we have three weeks. In my experience this is the average. Let us also assume that the play presents no unusual problems, and there is no reading beyond the first day. While we are assuming, let us add, for good measure, the assumption that a stage manager has laid out the floor plan with tape and provided furniture to approximate what we will be using.

A great deal has been written about blocking or staging. There are wonderful how-to-do-it charts to make those who love formulas very happy. My reaction to most of these systems is to say: "Yes, but suppose. . . . " My point is that there are no really valid rules. Center stage is indeed a good position, but only if the person occupying it is more interesting than someone who is on the side. I was discussing this problem once with the Canadian actor, Alan Scarfe, who gave me a good example. During the curtain call for *A Flea in Her Ear*, when Britain's National Theatre Company was touring, Laurence Olivier was way over on the side, having only played a very small role. Guess who had the focus of the audience's attention?

Good staging serves three principal functions: it provides the physical life of the characters the author has conceived; it creates focus; it augments the work of the designers in creating the visual style of the production.

Anyone who has heard good radio drama knows how much of a play can be communicated purely through sound. In the theater we have the responsibility of creating physical actions that should be better than those imagined by a radio listener and should illustrate the words of the playwright.

In contemporary plays, assuming that the setting and floor plan have been well thought out, staging is usually inevitable. Take a popular recent play, *The Subject Was Roses.* In almost every scene the physical activities are built into the script. Although the conflict between the characters is both specific and special, their activities are, for the most part, mundane household doings. The lines generally describe the stage business, and even where they do not, it is not hard to devise things to do in a Bronx apartment setting.

A play like *Tiger at the Gates,* on the other hand, is difficult to stage in an interesting manner. The action of the play is cerebral rather than physical. If you impose lots of business, you simply detract from the argument, which requires the full attention of the audience.

Even in so-called realistic plays, the blocking of a scene can never be completely real. In proscenium the actors "work" to the front of the house and will make sure that they face front when they have something important to say. In musicals they do this literally; in plays they should be in positions where they face a person downstage, that is someone looking at them from the same point of view as the audience. On a stage where the audience is on three sides of the actors, such as at both of New York City's Circles in the Square, the actors must be blocked in a more fluid manner. Whereas in proscenium theater the action will tend to be across the stage, in a three-quarter situation the action is at the diagonal. In the round the movement must be even more fluid. There is no position from which a face is visible to all the audience at the same time: center stage is the place from which only half the house can see an actor's face; standing with the back to the shortest aisle will provide the widest angle from which an actor can be seen.

As I have already mentioned, there is ample reading matter on the technicalities of blocking. I just wanted to make the point that the simulation of reality can be achieved only in relation to the kind of stage you are working on. I recently saw a proscenium production of *Old Times* in Canada. For the entire first act the three players remained seated. In real life this is perfectly feasible, given even the most dramatic situation. On the stage, however, it is boring to watch especially if, as was the case with this cast, the acting is soporifically dull.

It is always best when a director can give a motivation for a move. In the first act of *The Seagull* it is helpful to say to the actor playing Konstantin: "Go over to the lake and see if there is any sign of Nina's arrival when you say, 'If Nina is late it will spoil everything.' " But it is not very imaginative to say, "On the cue from Sorin, 'It's wonderful,' take six paces up left." The physical action is the same, but if the actor has no reason to make the move, it is just an arbitrary bit of blocking.

Sometimes you just have to be arbitrary in telling someone to move; and if the actor is clever, he will make it look natural. An intelligent performer knows that you have to clear entrances when they are about to be used, or that on a small stage an extreme separation between various characters may be necessary. If an actor is uncooperative, you can always resort to the apocryphal reply that Kazan is reputed to have given to the question, Why do I make this move? "Because you are being paid to." The academic equivalent is, "For your grade!"

STAGE BUSINESS

Moves and stage business are inexorably linked with character. In *The Seagull* Konstantin is a nervous person and moves a lot. Sorin, on the other hand, is placid and old, so he sits most of the time. The director must anticipate these facts in his preplanning, but should remain fluid enough to allow for character development in rehearsals. Sometimes an actor will come up with a piece of business that provides help to the other actors as well as himself. When I directed *Poor Bitos* in Los Angeles, the actor playing Robespierre in the play-within-the-play discovered that the real Robespierre used to eat oranges all the time. In the banqueting section this was wonderful, because it was not only something spidery for him to do with his fingers, it also created a genuine revulsion on the part of other characters as they reacted to the smell. (See fig. 8.)

In film the camera can always be pointing at whatever requires prominence. If we are shown an urn in close-up, we will remember it when later the detective is looking for the ashes. In the theater focus is harder to convey, because the audience is always looking at a "long shot." The obvious ways to command attention are levels, light, and prominent color or size. If an actor stands on a chair with everyone gathered around facing him, he has focus. If you fade in your scene very slowly and start the fade with a spotlight on that urn, the audience will get the idea.

I believe that creating focus by action is always more effective than technical devices. If you have a scene in which everyone is apprehensive of one character, then wherever he is on the stage, the other characters can keep the audience's attention on him by *always* relating to him with apprehension: for example, when his back is turned, they look at him fearfully and then quickly look away when he faces them. Tyrone Guthrie did this brilliantly in his production of *Henry VIII* that I have already referred to. In the scene where the Duke of Buckingham is betrayed by his surveyor, Guthrie had sixty of us—nobles, bishops, and other Shakespeareana—all looking away from this "Judas" as we left in small groups of two and three. It was the exact opposite of the classic focus-giving situation where Ginger Rogers is at the top of the staircase and on either side of her, top-hatted gentry have their arms held up to her.

If your actors are good, the focus will invariably be in the right place. The good actor automatically defers to the person who should be prominent. I will never forget rehearsing a tour of *Lord Pengo*, starring Walter Pidgeon (see fig. 6). An aged character man in the company played the butler. Whenever he entered, Pidgeon would always turn upstage to face him, so that the old gentleman had the focus and could get his laugh. When the actors are less good, you will have to direct them specifically to defer to the key figure.

Bad actors will often do anything to draw the attention to themselves. A first-rate actor in a poor company will receive the audience's interest no matter how self-effacing he tries to be. In that case you must either give him the lead or put him behind a pillar where he cannot take the attention away from your colorless principals.

If you stage a kitchen-sink play like *The Subject Was Roses,* it should all look as if it is happening spontaneously. The staging should not show. In other words, you aim at a theatrical realism. The opposite situation is staging a "comedy of manners" such as *The School for Scandal,* where the drawing room scenes should look formal, everything neatly in place, almost a ritual.

When I directed *Oedipus Rex* I felt that the choruses would gain in impact if they were ritualistically choreographed and juxtaposed against the main action, which was played with an approximation of reality, even though the actors wore masks. The device (not a particularly original one) was most effective.

The form of your overall blocking is one of your strongest directorial instruments. Between the two extremes I have just mentioned, there are many variations. Like so many things in directing, it is a matter of never losing sight of the overall effect that you want the production to make on the audience. If you stage *Oedipus Rex* like a cocktail party, it may be bizarre, but it will not have the ritual of Sophocles. On the other hand, if you stage *The Cocktail Party* like a ritual, you stand a better chance of being able to effect a marriage between Eliot's drawing room comedy dialogue and his borrowings from the drama of ancient Greece.

It is important to note that all these considerations should overlap. An actor playing a killer moves a lot because his character is nervous and tense. When he stabs his victim it is part of the plot. If he jumps up onto a piece of furniture to make his kill with a leap down, it can be focus-giving, in-character, and exciting.

"ROUGHING OUT" THE PLAY

I believe that the best method of blocking is to do the whole play roughly and quickly. Take short segments (i.e., from an entrance to the next exit), "rough" them out, and then repeat them. This procedure helps the actors to start relating to each other in their physical environment, and it helps you to get a feeling of the way that the production will move and flow. It also will give you a chance to make sure that your floor plans are really working. By "rough" I do not mean untidy, but simply the beginning of a form, with lots of room left for the actors to "breathe" in. With most plays, this process should not take more than three days.

DETAILED STAGING AND REHEARSING

After the play is "roughed out," you can start the detailed rehearsing of the scenes. I like to work scenes in order, but to avoid unnecessary waiting around for the company, you can take certain groups of characters who appear together and schedule all their scenes on one day. As an obvious example, if you are doing *Antony and Cleopatra,* you can schedule the Rome scenes in a block.

It is hard to know exactly how long you will need, but if you think a certain scene will take an hour, have the stage manager call the next scene for forty-five minutes later, because if you are through early, it is a pity to waste the last fifteen minutes. The essence of good rehearsing is to know when everyone has achieved all they are going to on a certain day. The law of diminishing returns applies more in the theater rehearsal than anywhere else I have been. Some producers and even stage managers get furious if you break early. They feel that they are not getting their money's worth. They do not understand that the psychological effect of letting people off twenty minutes early is worth far more than the results of slogging something out that simply needs to be taken home and thought about.

Before an actor can perform meaningfully, he must know several things about his role in the play: (1) who he is, (2) where he is, (3) when he is, (4) why he is, and (5) what he is doing.

The "who" is the character. If it is close to the actor himself, and the actor is at ease with himself, this is not a serious problem. Once I had an actor who was an obvious homosexual, playing the role of a "closet case." After a late run-through, he flabbergasted the entire cast by saying, "This man isn't queer, is he?" His performance was first-rate, and I realized to my horror that he was not aware of how successful he was in the role. To have been honest with him would have ruined his performance, so I replied, dishonestly, "Of course not!"

It is important to know the "where" of the play because the setting affects one's actions. We behave differently in a field than we do in the bedroom. We may do the same things in both places, but it is a different experience.

The "when": the period in time—not just the era but the time of year—also influences behavior. We behave differently from our forebears, that goes without saying, but we also vary our behavior and attitudes with the seasons. The cold in the last act of *The Seagull* is as important an element as the humidity in the first act.

The "why": if a play is any good, the characters will always have a good reason for being in a place at a given time. The most common theatrical device to gather people together is a social occasion; but even with the specifics of the gathering clarified, the actor must know why those particular characters have been invited and what their individual attitudes to the invitation are.

The "what": there is frequently a disparity between what people do and what is happening inside them. A woman receives a call from her lover who informs her that he is married. Inside she is hurt and heartbroken. What she does is say, "Let me put on the kettle. I need a cup of tea." The stage business is the creation of a pot of tea, but the audience must see the heartbreak from the demeanor of the unfortunate lady.

I know of no playwright whose work goes more fully into the complexities of human behavior than Anton Chekhov. In his plays, the subtext (that is, what is really going on inside the character) is as much a part of the play as the actual lines.

Here is the opening scene of *The Seagull*, which consists of a short conversation between two characters (see fig. 11). First I will reproduce the dialogue and stage directions as they appear in the script, then I will repeat it with the addition of all the things that would have to be arrived at by the director and the actors before it could be performed rather than just read. At the Moscow Arts Theater scripts annotated like this are called production scores.

ACT I

(A section of the park on Sorin's estate. It is dusk. Yakov & other workmen can be heard hammering on the stage which has been set up to one side. Masha and Medvedenko enter, returning from a walk.)

The play scene in Act I of *The Seagull*, Playhouse Theatre Company, Vancouver, B.C., 1965

Medvedenko: Why do you always wear black?

Masha: I'm in mourning for my life. I'm unhappy.

Medvedenko: But, why? . . . I am—I don't understand. . . . You're very healthy and, even though your father isn't rich, he's well provided for. Now I have a much harder life than yours. My salary is only twenty-three rubles a month and they take the pension fund out of that, but I don't go around in mourning. *(They sit.)*

Masha: Money is not important. I can be poor and still be happy.

Medvedenko: In theory maybe, but in practice it's a little different. Apart from me there are my two sisters, my mother and my little brother. We have to eat, and one must have tea . . . tobacco. On twenty-three rubles it's not easy.

Masha (looking around at the platform): The play will soon begin.

Medvedenko: Yes. Miss Zaretchny is going to act. The play is by Konstantin Gavrilovitch, you know. They're in love and today they will be united in their creative endeavors. You and I have nothing to unite us. I love you. I'm so miserable I just can't stay at home. Every day I walk the four miles here and then the four miles back and all I get from you is indifference. I can't say I blame you, I've no money and a big family to support. Who'd want to marry a man in that state?

Masha: Oh, please! *(Takes a pinch of snuff)* I'm touched by your love but I can't return it, that's all. *(Hands him the snuff box)*

Medvedenko: No thank you, I don't feel like it. *(Pause)*

Masha: Oh, it's stuffy here! There must be a storm on the way. . . . You're always talking about money. You seem to think that poverty is the worst thing that can happen to a person, but I would rather dress in rags and be a beggar. . . . Oh, what's the use! . . . You wouldn't understand. . . .

ACT I (Production Score)

As the house lights dim we hear from the stage the sound of hammering and crickets. The curtain goes up and we first of all become aware of a huge lake which we see in the background. Downstage of the lake a rough-hewn stage with a transparent white curtain has been erected; even now two workmen are hammering at it, but without any particular interest or enthusiasm. It is a hot summer night in rural Russia, 1896. (The photographs of Chekhov's country home near Yalta are my personal points of reference for the countryside and the architecture.)

Stage right is the house of Peter Sorin. Upstage left is the drive-way leading off the estate. There are chairs and benches set up facing the little stage.

A dog barks off to the left and the two workmen leave in the direction of the sound.

From the house we hear distant sounds of a rather theatrical laugh and we become aware that some kind of a party is in progress. In fact, Sorin's sister Arcadina and her lover Trigorin are visiting, and the steward, Shamraev, his wife Paulina, and their daughter Masha, together with her admirer, Medvedenko, have been invited to dinner.

After a few moments Masha comes on from the house, having slipped away from the party. She is tall and rather ungainly, but not unhandsome; she is dressed in black. A play by Konstantin is to be performed that night; she is in love with him, but her love is unrequited. She had hoped he might be working on his stage, but her disappointment soon gives way to her interest in the construction. She crosses to it and looks at it in silence, trying to imagine what the play will be like and maybe fantasizing about how she will find a new contact with Konstantin by her appreciation of his work.

Medvedenko appears, having also left dinner. He is shorter than she, a rather fussy, poorly dressed little man of thirty. He watches the tall, dark figure for a moment. He is struck by the blackness of the image with the long, black shadow that she makes.

Medvedenko: Why do you always wear black?

Masha turns on him, furious at having her reverie interrupted by the person she least wishes to see. We realize now that she has had a couple of drinks at dinner. She turns on him meaning to be hurtful.

Masha: I'm in mourning for my life. I'm unhappy.

Medvedenko is thrown by the directness of her answer and blurts out:

Medvedenko: But why?

Masha turns away from him and the stupidity of his question. Medvedenko tries to make himself clear; he is a schoolteacher and a pedantic one at that.

Medvedenko: I mean—I don't understand.

Masha turns to him as if she might explain, sparing him nothing. He counters her look with a little homily on the "what have you got to complain of" theme.

Medvedenko: You're very healthy and, even though your father isn't rich, he's well provided for.

He sees the annoyance his speech is producing in Masha and turns the subject to his favorite topic, his own poor lot, in an attempt to gain her sympathy.

Medvedenko: Now I have a much harder life than yours. My salary is only twenty-three rubles a month and they take the pension fund out of that, but I don't go around in mourning.

He sits on one of the chairs disconsolately. She comes over to him, towering above him. His attitude seems so materialistic and is utterly at odds with her idealism. She tries to explain.

Masha: Money is not important.

Medvedenko looks as if he might contradict her. She continues with increasing firmness.

Masha: I can be poor and still be happy.

Medvedenko gets up and starts a little lecture pointing at her with his finger to illustrate.

Medvedenko: In theory maybe, but in practice it's a little different. Apart from me there are my two sisters, my mother and my little brother. We have to eat, and one must have tea . . .

Masha turns from him in boredom and crosses back to the little stage. Medvedenko keeps going but starts to wind down.

Medvedenko: . . . tobacco. On twenty-three rubles it's not easy.

Masha is absorbed in the stage, but eventually turns to Medvedenko.

Masha: The play will soon begin.

Medvedenko is delighted to be included in her thoughts and goes over to her. He can never resist telling people things they already know.

Medvedenko: Yes. Miss Zaretchny is going to act. The play is by Konstantin Gavrilovitch, you know.

Masha looks at him amazed that he could not know how aware she is of this. Her look juxtaposed against the two names he has mentioned and their feeling for each other makes him speak with a romantic wishfulness.

Medvedenko: They're in love and today they will be united in their creative endeavors.

The wonder of this ideal relationship brings him back to the reality of his nonrelationship with Masha. He has sensed her feeling of envy at that which Nina is sharing with Konstantin.

Medvedenko: You and I have nothing to unite us.

She looks at him very sadly and not without pity. He misinterprets her look.

Medvedenko: I love you.

She does not reply, but turns and walks slowly away from him toward the driveway to see if Konstantin is coming yet. Medvedenko follows her like a small dog.

Medvedenko: I'm so miserable I just can't stay at home. Every day I walk the four miles here and then the four miles back and all I get from you is indifference.

Masha jumps up onto the stage to escape him and get into Konstantin's world. Medvedenko tries to get her sympathy by his self-denigration.

Medvedenko: I can't say I blame you, I've no money and a big family to support. Who'd want to marry a man in that state?

Masha cannot take this any more. She does the thing that she knows he hates and disapproves of. She noisily takes snuff as she turn to him.

Masha: Oh, please!

She sees the desperation in his eyes and jumps down beside him.

Masha: I'm touched by your love but I can't return it, that's all.

She offers him some snuff. It is a gesture of finality. He turns away from her rather prudishly.

Medvedenko: No, thank you, I don't feel like it.

She takes another noisy sniff and he turns to her as if he might express disapproval. She moves quickly away from him.

Masha: Oh, it's stuffy here! There must be a storm on the way.

He sits on the nearest chair and his dejection is pitiful. She sees him, and in spite of herself comes back for one last try.

Masha: You're always talking about money. You seem to think that poverty is the worst thing that can happen to a person, but I would rather dress in rags and be a beggar. . . .

She sees that he is uncomprehending and gives up, walking back to the driveway.

Masha: Oh, what's the use! . . . You wouldn't understand. . . .

There are, of course, many views of the same scene. The one above happens to be mine. Given two creative actors, I might alter some of the details, but not my overall view.

When Sidney Lumet made his movie of *The Seagull*, this scene opened with the two of them necking in the woods. Masha was petite and pretty, and Medvedenko was an attractive-looking youth.

It is the director's job to see that the actors have no unanswered questions that prevent them from playing their roles. One of the most helpful things a director can do for an actor is to provide the key for difficult transitions from one thought to another. There were several of these in the *Seagull* excerpt. When I directed the first Canadian production of *Fiddler on the Roof*, I arranged on the first day of rehearsal for the company to visit an Hasidic synagogue for some basic instruction in Judaic ritual and to have a question-and-answer session with the rabbi. The actor playing Mordcha, the character who is a sort of master of ceremonies at the wedding, asked the rabbi, "Why do I change from the pleasure of announcing the parental gifts of the candlesticks to the remembrance 'of our dear departed'?" The rabbi replied, "Because the mention of candlesticks on this sentimental occasion reminds you of your dead mother and the way she lit the candles at the Sabbath."

One of the most specific pieces of direction I ever heard was on the set for a television film. A young blond girl with more hair than acting talent was not reacting, in a scene, in the way the director wanted, so he said, "Hey Fluffy, try to make like you'se intelligent, which you'se ain't." A similar approach was the opening night of a Broadway flop that Laurence Olivier had directed. He went backstage during the intermission to give notes and all he said to his star, Charlton Heston, was, "Be better."

Some actors need little advice and will have figured out everything at home, just as the director should have. In North America, where the cult of the director has been encouraged, some actors prefer not to think about their role at all, but leave everything to the director. You may be lucky enough, however, to work with a resourceful actor like Tony Van Bridge who knows as much about Hobson in (what else?) *Hobson's Choice* as you ever will.

I suppose the secret of being helpful to actors is to know when to push and when to shut up and let them get on with it. From my observation, I would say that a lot of directors do too much "directing" and not enough listening, watching, suggesting, and enjoying. If a director is not showing his awareness and appreciation of the creativity and invention that is taking place before him, he may well destroy it. Actors who "give" in rehearsal are putting themselves in a vulnerable state. Acting depends greatly on the individual's confidence in his ability to play his role; the director must continually feed that confidence. One can be critical in rehearsal while still building up the actor's belief in himself. It is only rarely that a performer needs to be "put down" as part of the rehearsal process. Most actors, especially the good ones, balance on a razor's edge of confidence. If a director upsets this balance, he is likely to be the one who will eventually have to restore it.

Some directors launch into an actor at the beginning of rehearsals, sometimes with very sound suggestions, and suddenly find themselves, a week before opening, with a human jelly on their hands. Then they have to spend the rest of rehearsal having to put Humpty Dumpty together again, frequently at the expense of the whole production. One must be careful in gauging just how much direction an actor can absorb at a given time.

I frequently become quite attached to my actors during rehearsals and particularly devoted to my leading ladies. Good rehearsals are, to me, one of the higher forms of love-making. I once discussed this with Michel Saint-Denis and he said my devotion to actresses was perfectly normal, then adding in his inimitable French accent, "Zee time to worry eez when it does not 'appen to you."

PACE

One of the things that people always seem to pick on when discussing the work of a director is "pace." When a critic likes a show, he will often say something like, "The production maintained a good pace."

Pacing does not mean simply speed. The snail's pace at which so many plays proceed certainly makes one long to yell, "Faster. Pick up your cues!" But pacing means variety. Breakneck speed for three acts can be nearly as boring as an evening of pauses and grunts.

The key to pacing is introducing each new idea dynamically and playing at the pace that is appropriate to the action. The more variety of pace that you and your actors can achieve, the more the audience will enjoy themselves.

The dynamics of pace are inexorably linked with the creation of mood and atmosphere, as I hope *The Seagull* excerpts have indicated. The director should, therefore, be working with his actors on this aspect of the production as soon as he starts detailing the scenes. The director's work is similar to that of a good orchestral conductor. The main difference is that whereas the maestro is up there in front of his players at the premiere brandishing his baton, the director is likely to have fled to the bar for a brandy.

The worst moment in rehearsals for me is when it becomes apparent that I have miscast an actor. The special quality that he brought to the readings turns out to be merely a façade. The romantic hero is actually a marshmallow. The uninhibited girl I cast as the trollop is now wearing a crucifix and is constantly pulling her skirt down.

In Los Angeles, I cast a noted "second banana" in a part that required amusing exchanges with the audience. Two weeks into rehearsals I found out that he was desperately trying to live down that image in Hollywood and wanted to be considered a serious older leading man. The producer suggested we replace him; I was wrong in not agreeing. When you have made a mistake in casting, and everybody does, it is much fairer to all concerned to admit it and make a change.

When I was directing stock packages, that is, tours that travel in the summer through resort areas, I would sometimes be given a "star" who was considered "box office" simply because of exposure on television panel shows. On these occasions I had to be totally realistic and rely on the supporting cast to cover up the lead's deficiencies—that was the name of the game. The director, George Keathley, told me of a time he was tearing his hair over a disastrously miscast star and Luther Adler said, "Relax, George, you can't make pineapples out of shit!"

IMPROVISATIONS

In this day when more and more theatrical evenings consist of lines written by the actors, we must certainly discuss improvisations. If a relationship is simply not jelling in rehearsal, you can sometimes help by setting up an imagined situation for the characters, preferably two at a time. These situations should either be very close to the scene in the play or very different—nothing halfway. Also, unless you go immediately back into the text, improvisations can be dangerous because they create an independence from the author's work which may negate the finished result. Improvisation is more effective when you know the actors well. Improvising is a release for some and an inhibiting experience for others. The important thing to remember is that an invented scene working well can never be a substitute for the author's play fully realized. I have found that in rehearsing plays that come under the category of Theater of the Absurd, improvisational situations for the characters are enormously valuable. The transitions in this kind of drama can be hair-raisingly difficult, so it is doubly essential that the actors completely own the characters they play. When I did *The Knack* in Vancouver, B.C., Neil Dainard, Hutchinson Shandro, and John Juliani were always coming up with wonderful inventions for their characters (see fig. 7).

Stage managers often ask me when I want the actors to drop their scripts. I feel that responsible actors should know their own speed. I am not concerned if people carry scripts for the entire first week. It is better than having them waste everyone's time by continually yelling for prompts. However, if an actor is using the script as a crutch, like dark glasses, then you must simply remove it and try to boost the actor's confidence as well as finding better ideas and imagery for him to work with. Incidentally, when actors with large roles are struggling with the text, you should always try to leave them alone directorially until they regain the security that they had before they dropped the script. Noel Coward solved this problem by insisting that all his actors arrive at the first rehearsal word-perfect. Understandably many actors, particularly in method-land, found this both difficult and intimidating. As I have discovered, to my cost, drama students have to be given deadlines for learning. The competition with sex, term papers, politics, and pot is simply too strong.

RUN-THROUGH

About halfway into rehearsals, I have a run-through of sorts. I used to call them ''stumble-throughs,'' until I got the term ''grope-through'' from Ed Payson Call. These ''grope-throughs'' give me a chance to step back and see what has and has not been achieved, and where the work now needs to be concentrated.

By this time, of course, our ideal stage manager has furnished us with rehearsal props. We may even have some of the sound effects, which will affect timing and must be as carefully coordinated into the performance as everything else. One of the most important precepts that I learned at the Old Vic School was that the man who rings "the bell that summons me to heaven or hell" is as important a creative artist at the moment the bell rings as the actor playing *Macbeth*.

The thing I hate the most about rehearsal run-throughs is that I am so close to the actors while I am whispering notes to an assistant (which I have to do, as I cannot read my own writing). Director Jay Broad suggests that one get up on a table, so at least one has the distance of height. This is a good idea, but of course the sooner you get into the theater, at this stage, the better.

The trauma of moving from tiny room to big theater is one of the nightmares of directing. So often something has life and excitement in the rehearsal room, only to lose it when it gets onto the stage. As Seattle's Duncan Ross has observed in my hearing, "There are no small actors, only small rehearsal rooms." The point being that the actors, without realizing it, have come to believe in the rehearsal room as the place where the play is taking place. They have become used to your reaction at close quarters. When you move into the theater, you can ease the shock of the whole thing by moving away from the stage gradually.

In the case of arena staging, you must rehearse in a room large enough for you to move around. The best way of introducing actors to this experience is for the director to keep altering his vantage point. I will always remember blocking *The Best Man* for the Playhouse-in-the-Park in Philadelphia. Ruth McDevitt was re-creating her role of the club woman, Mrs. Gamadge. When her first entrance came up, she trotted to the sofa and planted herself there, as if to say to me, "That's where I sat on Broadway, young man, and that's where I'm going to sit here." I did not say anything to her, but just walked around behind her. After a moment she noticed that I was no longer in front of her and she started looking around. When she eventually saw me sitting behind her, she said, "Oh, my God, it's the round, isn't it?" From that moment she deferred to me most graciously.

Directing a Musical

I once heard Abe Burrows say that when you direct a musical you become primarily an executive. I know what he meant. A musical usually has a shorter rehearsal period because, with so many people involved, it is much more expensive. Also, as there are really three people directing simultaneously, more should be accomplished in a shorter time. It is a different experience from rehearsing a play.

THE DIRECTOR, CHOREOGRAPHER, AND MUSICAL DIRECTOR

Normally the director is responsible for the overall production and will stage the book, that is, the nonmusical scenes. The musical director does just what his title implies. He rehearses all the singing and the orchestra, as well as directing the music from the orchestra pit during the performance. The choreographer does the musical numbers and the dances. Some directors do some of the musical numbers, especially if they have a background in dancing or choreography, as the most successful directors of musicals have.

This whole question of division of responsibility can be a problem. When I directed a production of *Most Happy Fella*, in which all but one speech is sung, I was somewhat surprised to read on the program that musical staging and choreography were the work of the lady who did the dances! Similarly, if the choreographer has done all the numbers, the credit, "choreography by . . . " is insufficient. The thing to do is to agree beforehand on who will do what, and then make sure the credits are accurate. If you are not a choreographer, it can be a mistake to try to do complicated musical staging. The same goes for sword fights and acrobatic sequences in all productions. Badly staged fights can be dangerous both to the audience and to the actors. It is much better, and safer, to get a specialist in to handle stage business that requires specific expertise. Of course, interludes involving magical tricks, flying sequences, and such must all be in keeping with the production as a whole. I think some directors are afraid that they will lose face if they cannot do everything. In my opinion, they lose much more when they try to take on something that they really cannot handle.

PLANNING

In no area of theatrical endeavor is the stage manager more important than in a musical. To coordinate three sets of rehearsals simultaneously, while keeping everyone on schedule all the time, is a major undertaking.

A good way to plan things is to divide every scene into subscenes. Take what is probably the most popular musical ever created, *Fiddler on the Roof*. The prologue begins outside Tevya's house: the Fiddler is, of course, on the roof; Tevya comes forward and starts his soliloquy. Halfway through this the entire cast enters (the villagers) and begins the number "Tradition." When the number is over, we begin scene 1, which is set in the kitchen of Tevya's house. The first part of the scene is between Golde, the wife, and her five daughters. Three and a half pages later, Golde is left conveniently alone for a scene with Yente, the Matchmaker, which is momentarily interrupted by Motel, the Tailor, who is the suitor of Tzeitel, the oldest daughter. After Yente's departure Tzeitel comes in to find out what has transpired, and Golde leaves the stage rather than tell her. Hodel and Chava, the other two older daughters, come in to hear the news, and there is a short conversation, which prepares us for the famous trio, "Matchmaker, Matchmaker."

For rehearsal purposes this will break down as follows:

Prologue A: The soliloquy (which the director will have rehearsed with Tevya alone)

Prologue B: The number, "Tradition," which should be done by the choreographer and the director (the latter would be involved whatever the circumstance, because there are lines of dialogue interspersed in the song)

Scene 1A: The scene between Golde and her daughters

Scene 1B: Begins as the last girl leaves and Yente enters

Scene 1C: Begins with Tzeitel's entrance and ends with the number, "Matchmaker, Matchmaker"

The sample rehearsal schedule on the following page covers the prologue and first scene of *Fiddler* and utilizes time in an unwasteful manner. It might seem unnecessary to list the artists' names, but it is best to make your call sheets absolutely foolproof.

This schedule is easy to follow, and it insures a good use of time. If you are doing resident stock, and you only have five hours of rehearsal with the Equity people, you can frequently arrange a schedule that gives you a total of eight or nine hours of work simply by calling some people at a later hour, and dismissing others earlier. But as the musical director has to conduct another show at night, it can be a little hard on him if he has to work a long day as well.

SIDES

I do not believe there is much point in having a reading for a musical, unless it is a new one. There is one problem that often arises, however. The people who handle the rights tend to send "sides" for most roles (that is, sheets that just give the cue and then the line). As these cues are frequently single words such as "Yes" or "Oh!" one often gets an excited line from a chorus boy thrown in every time some other character says "Yes" or "Oh!" In England, Equity banned the use of these pernicious apologies for scripts for all their members. I wish our unions here would make the same stand. They are an abomination that clearly reveal the mercenary insensitivity of some of the people who handle the rights for what are in many cases minor works of art.

BLOCKING

On the first day of rehearsal, I like to block the whole show with the choreographer beside me, so he can see how my stage move-

REHEARSAL SCHEDULE

PRODUCTION Fiddler On the Roof

DATE	TIME	LOCATION	SCENE	DESCRIPTION	DIRECTION	CHARACTERS		
8-1-72	10 AM 11:30	STAGE	IC	"Match-maker"	Choreographer Accompanist	Tzeitel (Smith)	Hodel (Brown)	Chava (Klein)
" "	"	Lobby	IB	Yente visits	Director	Yente (Schwartz)	Golde (Shore)	(Tzeitel and Motel not called)
" "	10 AM	PIT		Musical Numbers	Musical Director	Tevya (Hart)		
	" 11:30	"		"	"	Motel (José)		
"	" 11:30	Wardrobe		Fitting	Costume Designer	Tevya (Hart)		

ment will mesh with his numbers. If something is awkward for him, we can compromise then and there. That way the whole thing will fit together at the first run-through.

I have usually enjoyed wonderful relationships with my colleagues in musicals. The loneliness of the director is happily eliminated when there is a congenial triumvirate. I have noticed, however, that choreographers frequently feud with the musical directors, particularly over the matter of tempi.

THE CHORUS

A word about the chorus which applies to all crowd scenes in and out of musicals. If one takes the time to give each person a character and build relationships between them, the mass entrances and exits will have much greater reality. The chorus will also feel more important and contribute more. I found this worked even when staging opera, although I knew that the resident staff thought I was crazy to take the time.

A director accustomed only to plays must beware of being too realistic in his direction of the book. The scenes are usually written in very broad strokes, and the "point" is arrived at quickly. The performers are frequently nonactors, and the theaters are often huge, so that subtlety is out. The thing to remember is that, in a good musical, all the climactic moments are done in song and dance, so if the spoken scenes can bridge the musical numbers entertainingly, then you have not failed in your direction.

One last word of advice to those attempting their first musical. When you stage the curtain call, do not forget to arrange an acknowledgment for the conductor from the cast. I omitted this when I did my first big musical and unnecessarily offended Maestro Philip Fradkin, a most efficient and helpful musical director with whom I have now worked on six productions.

 **Visitors Attending Rehearsals**

When is a rehearsal not a rehearsal? When there is a visitor. Actors choose their calling because they like to perform for people, and when someone new appears at rehearsals, they will invariably start showing off. If they are insecure, they will become more so. You may be permitting an actor to do something wrong in rehearsals for a variety of good reasons, but a visitor dropping into rehearsal does not understand this; he may form an erroneous opinion of the work in hand and, worse still, offer thoroughly damaging advice to the actor after rehearsal.

Some visitors are poker-faced; if you are doing a comedy, the actor will think, "Oh God! It's not funny!" But the reverse can happen and be just as bad. A dizzy lad from wardrobe comes in to arrange a fitting and lingers, laughing, while a special favorite executes a piece of comic business. After he has left, it can be hard to convince the actor that this mirth is not a particularly good barometer by which to gauge an audience on opening night.

The worst visitors are those who are totally unknown to the cast. Most theater people are slightly paranoid in the first place; in rehearsals we are doubly so. I once did an awful play in Los Angeles with Doris Roberts in the cast. People were always dropping into rehearsals (the Hollywood Syndrome). Whenever she spotted a stranger, Doris would sidle up to me and say, "Is that my replacement?" I think in the case of this play it was wishful thinking.

65

When I was running the Vancouver Playhouse, we had a policy that worked very well. At the first reading, most of the production staff would attend (my theory being that an occasion that is already horrendous cannot be made any worse by being shared). As the producer, I would not usually return before two weeks into the three-week rehearsal, when I would arrange with the director to attend a run-through so that there was something for me to see. I would never discuss the event with anyone but the director. If actors cornered me, I would simply say something noncommittal, but never discouraging, and remind them that the director was their barometer. If it was a comedy or a new play, we would frequently invite a few outside people to attend—preferably not other actors, and never relatives. This induced a good kind of nervousness in the actors and started to break the exclusivity of the rehearsal.

Publicity people tend to be noisy rehearsal visitors because they invariably bring program biographies and things that the actors quite rightly are concerned about. Here the stage manager is the one who sets the tone. If he is in command of his domain, the staff knows that interruption will not be countenanced. If he is not in control, then it is up to you to find suitable epithets to clear the room of unwanted guests.

TRY-OUTS AND PREVIEWS

Try-outs and previews are a trial for the director, as far as "advice" is concerned. Everyone knows how to fix the show! If they are knowledgeable people, the director will usually listen; but he simply must not lose his overall viewpoint. The opinions are invariably contradictory, so the sum total of the advice is likely to be zero in value. One wonders why, if the man from the William Morris Agency is so full of ideas, he has not become a director. (Incidentally, at least two have, which only strengthens my point regarding those who have not.)

This story sums up the absurdity of the situation for me: I was sitting at a semipublic dress rehearsal in Florida when a well-known personal manager came up to me and whispered in my ear, "That girl's great. . . . " A long pause followed, during which I hoped he would take the hint and leave. He then added in a worried pianissimo, "Isn't she?"

Novices are particularly vulnerable to unconstructive criticism. I recently asked one of my graduate students how his rehearsals were coming along. He had had a run-through the day before, which two people from another project had attended. He said their attitude and what they had relayed to his cast had shaken his confidence in his production and demoralized his company. This kind of thing happens all too often, especially on campus, and is frequently the result of jealousy.

In a school where the only consideration should be the learning experience, one wants as many people to share the rehearsal as possible. I always insist, however, that observers must arrive at the beginning of a session and remain until it is over. It is also a good idea to tell students that they should not seek advice from their friends or even other faculty members until the play has closed.

Anyone who goes into college theater to avoid back-biting professionals is in for a big disappointment. From my observation the maliciousness that often accompanies campus productions makes Sardi's seem like vespers in a quiet cathedral.

Technical Rehearsals

The rehearsals have now, theoretically, progressed through the logical sequence: reading; blocking; exploration of motivation and movement; clarifying details of business; running scenes, acts, and finally the whole play. If you have been lucky, you will have had a week of rehearsal on the stage; but in most situations the stage is not available until the technical rehearsals.

The most common problem I run into at this point is that when actors arrive at the appointed time, they find stagehands still working on the set. The stage manager should never let this happen, and it is his responsibility to see that everything is ready on time. You must try to do as much work as possible with the technical people before the cast gets on the set. If the director has been shown the furniture, props, and set pieces beforehand, many problems can be anticipated and solved prior to the arrival of the actors. I like to sit with the lighting designer at a rehearsal room run-through and go over ideas at the end of each scene, so that he can then have his lighting plot ready prior to the first technical rehearsal in the theater.

COSTUME PARADE

A costume parade should always be held early enough to allow sufficient time for alterations to be made before the first dress rehearsal. Some strong light is required for this. I get out front with the costume designer and someone to take notes. You should always make three copies of the costume notes—for the director, the designer, and the stage manager—to preclude bickering later over what changes were to be made. The actors should come out singly, walk around a bit, and try anything physical that they are going to do in the costume. If an actress does not care for a costume and wants it changed, she may deliberately model it in such a way that it will look dreadful. You will frequently have to exercise considerable firmness, especially as the objections are often based on personal prejudices, such as "My boyfriend doesn't like me in yellow." I did a production not long ago with a young actress who weighed at least two hundred fifty pounds. She tried every way to get her costume changed because she felt her gown, a flattering muu-muu, made her look fat.

DRESS REHEARSAL

In these final rehearsals on stage, I like to try to do things gradually with the actors and the crew. The first time through the play, I let the actors wear their street clothes and stop as often as they want to, so they can get used to working on the set. You should have sound cues immediately, because they will affect the timing. The lighting people can try some of the cues, but I do not normally expect the lighting plot to be completely realized at this early stage.

For the first run-through in costume, there is no point in wearing makeup. It simply dirties the clothes, and if the lighting is not finished, there is nothing valuable for a director to comment on. If an actor is wearing a beard, however, he should start working with it as soon as possible. In this run-through you should try not to stop, because the actors who have costume changes need to try them in the actual time they will have during the performance. In all these rehearsals, the director's aim should be to help the company become comfortable and relaxed, so they can start performing the play as quickly as possible with the minimum of worry. Speaking of worry, be sure to tell them that the lighting is not finished; otherwise, they will be searching for "hot spots" and will be worried about not having their faces seen.

When the lighting is complete, it is time for a full dress rehearsal with makeup, and the director now has the opportunity to see the show as a whole. If all the planning has been good, and everyone has done his job, the result will have a unity of style. If the doorway is too narrow for the crinoline or the chair breaks under the weight of an ingénue such as the one I described earlier, then the carpenter has a lot of last-minute work to do.

In the case of a new play, you may find yourself demanding a whole new setting to accommodate a rewrite. I have seen shows on Broadway where a set clearly did not belong in the original concept. It was obvious that the designer had had to effect a hasty compromise in his original work.

PREVIEWS

My feelings regarding preview audiences are mixed. If you are doing a comedy or a new play, audience reactions are invaluable. One preview full of friends, however, can be totally misleading. In regional theater particularly, the social set likes to attend openings, and they have frequently overimbibed for the ordeal. The contrast between the "Gin and Geritol" set and the friendly folk of the preview can be most unnerving. I think that unless there are two previews, it is better not to have any at all. When there are three or four, or a whole try-out period, then the production can become really polished. The only exception is a show that is no good: it will simply get worse during previews as everyone realizes that the swan has now revealed itself as the goose it always was.

One last thing to guard against: some Shakespeare festivals give extended performances for school children before the press opening. A director must insist on some adult previews as well, because the difference between a high school audience and a "social" first night can completely destroy the actors' morales.

THE DAY OF THE OPENING

On the day of the opening, I am a firm believer in calling the company in. I think it is less nerve-racking for the performers to be together during that day of ordeal rather than to charge around town trying to kill time. I have tried many forms of opening day rehearsal, and I have finally arrived at the format that seems to work best. I call the actors in at a time that will make it possible for them to leave the theater area before the show. If the final dress rehearsal has finished late, I give my notes on the opening day.

The rehearsal is then a relaxed (you hope) walk-through of the play in street clothes, but with all the technical things operative. This is simply a gentle charging of the acting batteries.

OPENING NIGHT

I abhor the hysteria of New York openings. Actors should be sitting peacefully in their dressing rooms, not distracted by successions of deliveries from well-wishers. They know it is opening night from their queasy stomachs and their trembling hands without being reminded of the fact every few minutes. A few seasons ago Brian Bedford made a huge success on Broadway in *School for Wives*. The opening was also his birthday. About fifteen minutes before the curtain went up, the cast decided to surprise him with a cake and sung greetings. After he had cut into the cake someone asked him what he had wished for and he replied: "I'm awfully grateful to you, but I do wish you would all leave my dressing room."

There is a popular notion that an opening night performance is the actor's best. I have rarely found this to be the case. There are a few performers who seem to rise to the occasion with a whole new energy, but it is optimistic to expect that kind of miracle, so beloved of the old "show biz" movies, from normal human beings. I have found, though, that musicals tend to go better on opening night than plays. I think perhaps the orchestra gives an enormous shot of adrenalin to everyone.

All directors hate openings. A common nightmare among us is that we will interrupt a scene while the audience is there. I love audiences. After all, their responses and approval are what we are working for, and their box office dollars keep the theaters open. I find it hard, however, not to feel hostile to the noisy first-night crowd, who treat the occasion as a social reunion rather than a theatrical event. The worst place for this is Palm Beach, where the actors are called at 8:45 for the half hour, even though the curtain is announced for 8:30 P.M. Directors there are urged to instruct their actors to go fast, so the customers can get back to the bar as quickly as possible, and to act loudly so they can be heard over the rattle of jewelry and the incessant society chatter.

Critics

Provided that the director has maintained his position in the driver's seat through the opening night, the company will be measuring their work against the yardstick of his judgment. If there is a try-out or there have been previews, and he has correctly gauged the audience reaction, his position will be so strong that the performers will not even be confused by the "helpful comments" of the cognoscenti who love to get backstage before an opening and destroy morale. In both of Gordon Davidson's theater groups in Los Angeles, the preview audiences appeared to be made up almost entirely of actors who had been turned down in preliminary auditions. But it is after the curtain has come down on opening night that the creative people really become sitting targets.

Critics are important to the theater because the public likes to be told what to see. They do not necessarily follow the advice, but they like to hear the voice. A critic once told me that the frustration of his life was that he knew he could kill a show, but he also knew that he could not persuade people to go unless they wanted to.

In major centers like New York, San Francisco, Los Angeles, Chicago, and Boston, there are enough critics to ensure that a production gets a cross section of critical opinion. In smaller cities—and they are the cities where the good regional theaters tend to be—it is another story. In these places the same man usually handles the symphony, opera, ballet, and the theater, to say nothing of chamber music and the odd visit to the movies. Only a true Renaissance man has the background to be expert in all these fields, whereas these reviewers (one could hardly call them critics) are frequently people who have been demoted from the sports page. This is *not* just one of those things that people say; it really does happen. How seriously should experienced theater people take these notices?

A tenor friend of mine once sang in a production of *The Barber of Seville* in San Francisco and was most upset to receive a terrible review in one of the papers. He called his teacher, Robert Weede, in search of solace. Weede said to him: "How long did you work to prepare that role?" The tenor estimated that it was all of a year. Weede asked: "Do you think you know anything about the part?" The tenor replied that he did. Weede then said: "How long do you think that critic spent studying the score and your part in it?" The tenor got the point, and Weede then said: "Okay, were you bad or good? You are the one who should know. Why do you need to read the paper to find out?"

If you are directing a play in a city where you know that the local critic is hostile to the theater (many of them are affiliated with amateur groups and wage constant warfare on professionals), then you should warn the company of this. If they have any real security, they will not read that critic anyway. But how many of us really have enough sense to kill our curiosity?

If you are working with students, you must urge them not to be affected either by praise or abuse, because they can be seriously influenced by what they read in print. I find the idea of reviews for college shows to be absolutely ridiculous, but I am in the minority. I do not think that kind of publicity has a place in the educational process. The public, amazingly, still tends to believe what they read in print. Anybody who has ever been involved in a news story, and then reads the press account, will know how foolish that is. It is, unfortunately, very hard to make young people understand this and persuade them that printed words are capable of being as unreliable and irrelevant as spoken words. The strange paradox is that they accept this principle when it is an endorsement of a political candidate they dislike; but when it is a notice of a play they are doing, they start taking their press seriously.

Some directors acquire a good, unconcerned attitude regarding the press, and then when the show is a critical success, the same people read their reviews to everyone. A few weeks later, when they have been panned for another production, they are on rather weak ground when they start saying things like: "What do the critics know?"

I have done very few productions with which I was completely happy, but two of my best experiences were certainly *Peer Gynt* (see fig. 10) and *Next Time I'll Sing to You*. Here are excerpts from two reviews of each.

From *The Hollywood Reporter*, 3 June 1966, on the Theatre Group production of *Next Time I'll Sing to You*:

> Theatre Group, playing its last season in its home and birthplace, UCLA, has a funny, antic, meaningful play to open its current season, James Saunders' "Next Time I'll Sing to You." With this British play, of the comedy of the absurd school, Theatre Group again establishes its vitality and its distinctive personality: contemporary, bold, progressive. Malcolm Black, a visiting director, has staged the work with vigor and control, building the rather formless material to shape and cumulative power. It is another hit for Theatre Group. . . .
>
> Saunders writes exceptionally beautiful language. It is funny in a sharp, modern way. It is also remarkably poetic without the least pretension. His imagery is particularly original and moving. The actors employ a variety of English speech patterns, Oxonian, Midlands, American stage English. It is not haphazard, but purposeful. To quote again, one actor says at one point, "We're not here to enjoy ourselves." And so we're not, actor or audience. As in the best and rarest theatre, all are there to learn, and do so, in "Next Time I'll Sing to You," with laughter and with tears and with a sense of being part of something that is not only theatre but life itself.
>
> — Jim Powers

From *Variety*, 3 June 1966:

> English playwright James Saunders, author of this literary absurdity, has cast his net of well woven language into a sea of metaphysical fishes but has come up with no dramatic whale. So much for metaphor, of which this remarkably auditory evening abounds. . . .
>
> Malcolm Black's direction gives no overall style to the produc-

tion, except that of austerity. The stage sets of Sydney Rushakoff are sparse with only skeletal pieces, the arc lights remain nakedly in view and there is no music. Costumes by Diana Polsky and lighting by Myles Harmon contributed to the cerebral mood. . . .

From *The Vancouver Sun*, 6 January 1967:

PEER GYNT BRILLIANTLY DONE BY A TOP
NOTCH STAGE TEAM
by David Watmough
Sun Drama Critic

With Canada precisely the same age this year as Ibsen's massive masterpiece, "Peer Gynt," the decision of The Playhouse Theatre Company to mount this exhaustive meditation on the nature of the self, in 1967, was an extremely felicitous one.

In the event, the nearly 3½ hour interplay of fantasy and vestigial reality encompassing the life of a Norwegian villager was brilliantly justified, and the capacity audience at Thursday night's opening seemed thoroughly subjugated by Malcolm Black's swift and imaginative direction. . . .

"Peer Gynt," it must be flatly stated, is for the men rather than the boys. But given the disposition to enjoy great theatre most ably presented, The Playhouse's New Year offering must surely be without equal across Canada.

Malcolm Black, I find, is one of those maverick directors whom it is awfully difficult to pin down as far as the kind of play he seems to be happiest with.

One moment he is all flair and insight with a modern satiric comedy, the next we have him equally at home with a redoubtable classic—as with this "Peer Gynt" where he manages a highly acceptable balance between proper respect for the work and an equally necessary awareness of a modern audience's need. . . .

The performance of Neil Dainard in the title role must surely go down in the annals of thespian history on the West coast as an interpretation which is individual in contour, fetching in content, and thoroughly credible throughout.

From *The Province*, 6 January 1967:

Not Ibsen
CREDIBILITY WAS LACKING
by James Barber

The Playhouse Theatre Company production of Peer Gynt which opened last night is dominated by a very simple, very strong monolithic set, which appears to have influenced everything else on stage and created a flat almost two dimensional story. . . .

I was not impressed. The play, as written, and sometimes played, is a great favorite of mine. I am favorably prejudiced towards it, even before it opens, but last night's Peer Gynt, despite its moments of imagination and originality in conception, lacked motivation and credibility.

There were times when, had I not been convinced that I was watching a class B movie, I would have compared the stage with one of the Bob Hope "Road to . . . . " films. . . .

Neil Dainard, as Peer, dominates the stage like a giant among pygmies. But the Scandinavian sterility is almost too much for him. Ibsen was one of the first stage writers to fully concern himself with the why of people, and Malcolm Black's direction appeared determined to ignore it.

These excerpts of notices may help to explain why I, as a director, am not greatly affected by reviews. As a producer, on the other hand, I am deeply concerned with what is written because, unfortunately, it affects the box office. But the reviews that have annoyed me most have been those that have praised work I know to be inferior.

Professional actors tend to acknowledge publicly only the reviews that are complimentary. In private many bleed for years from personal remarks written by people like John Simon, Claudia Cassidy, and the late Nathan Cohen of Toronto.

I must say that I would far rather be a director than a critic. As a director you can, from time to time, share an experience with a group of people that is totally rewarding. As a critic you can achieve considerable power, especially if you are on the *New York Times*. You can coin an insult that may pass into the language; but you will always be denied a part in the creative process and seldom even have the rewards of an audience member who can submit to an experience and enjoy himself without having to think up things to say for a speedily written report.

Critics have sometimes rendered great service to the theater by leading public taste. In recent years Harold Hobson of the London *Sunday Times* championed Harold Pinter when nobody else in the press wanted to know about him. When Kenneth Tynan, in a now-famous phrase, said of *Look Back in Anger*, "I doubt if I could love anyone who did not wish to see *Look Back in Anger*. It is the best young play of its decade," he pushed the London audience into accepting *The Angry Young Men*. In New York City, the critics tend to judge works by applying the yardstick of popular public taste. They give, as it were, the consumer report. In regional theater, critics like Cecil Smith in Los Angeles and Christopher Dafoe, first in Winnipeg and now in Vancouver, have done a great deal to help the theater, principally by taking it seriously and advising the public to do likewise.

When George Bernard Shaw, perhaps the most famous critic of all time, retired from drama criticism, the refreshingly honest Mrs. Patrick Campbell is reported to have said: "We pretended he was not serious, but our fingers trembled as we turned to his articles. A good riddance, but how we shall miss what he might have said about the others!"

Going Back to See Your Productions

Many directors hate going back to see their productions, and in many cases, I do not blame them. However, it is a responsibility that cannot be dodged. If the actors are prepared to go in night after night to perform in the event that you have had a good hand in shaping, the least you can do is join them from time to time. One of the advantages of being a resident director at a theater, or a resident in the city where your show is playing, is that you can pay regular visits to your production.

One performance that you should never miss is the second night. First of all, you will need to reassure those whom the critics have disliked and, in some cases, to curb the excessive excitement caused by misplaced praise. Second-night performances are traditionally anticlimactic. If the cast knows that you are there, they are more likely to overcome their hangovers from the opening night party.

If the production is a good one, you stand a fair chance after a week of performance of seeing the show the way you wanted it. In the case of a comedy, you had better get back before a month is out, because there will doubtless be many "improvements." Audiences at comedies are treacherous creatures, because they seduce the actors into excess and then resent the fact that their demands have been submitted to.

George Abbott in his autobiography has said that actors are at their best when a show is a failure and at their worst when it is a success. Certainly "the divine discontent" of the artist is nowhere more apparent than in the actor. One is always hearing sad tales of the boredom and frustration of the "long run." I have always thought that it must be preferable to the unemployment line, but apparently it is not. Some of the shows I have seen in New York City have appalled me with their sloppiness. A director who is going to pocket a big royalty check each week should certainly be prepared to take an occasional look at the production that bears his name. In the case of a big hit that runs long enough to require cast replacements, the audience will frequently be watching a company of actors who have never even met the director, let alone had a rehearsal with him.

I have already mentioned the importance of giving the stage manager the respect of his office. I believe that notes after the opening should, ideally, be given through him. They should at least be given in his presence. By giving direction without him after the opening, you are undercutting his authority.

One of the worst things about going back to a production, especially when it is a hit, is the tale-telling and name-calling that goes on. One actor will complain that an actress is spoiling his laugh by faulty timing of the feed line. An actress will complain that her leading man has halitosis, and so on. In most instances I have a standard reply: "Tell the stage manager." If you are paying regular visits, you have already noted any infringements in the actual playing. If the stage manager is any good (and if he is not, your show will deteriorate), he is perfectly capable of handling personal complaints.

The saddest story I have ever heard from a conscientious stage manager concerned a tour of a musical about a man with five daughters. The girls all complained that when "Dad" kissed them, he was doing it on the lips in a distinctly unfatherly fashion. Whenever the stage manager tried to remonstrate with said incestuous father, the "star" playing the role would lock himself in his dressing room. My friend, the stage manager, made the right decision, I believe. He quit the show.

 # The Hard Facts of Directing as a Profession

The question I am most frequently asked about directing is "How do I become a director?" Considering how few opportunities there are, it is amazing how many people want to try it. An examination of the backgrounds of the directors you admire will not provide the answer. People become directors in all kinds of ways (some of which would require an X rating to describe). I have fairly strong feelings about the kind of preparation that a person should undergo before he presumes to lead a group of artists. On the other hand, there are some successful directors who have done none of these things.

I believe that the more activities a director can have experienced for himself around the theater, the better he will be able to coordinate them when guiding a production himself. I have already explained the advantage of a background in stage management. Just as important is some experience of acting in front of an audience. You are far less likely to mishandle actors if you have experienced some of the agonies for yourself.

It is an advantage for a director to have had a fairly good education if he wishes to work with anything but contemporary material. One has enough homework to do with a period play without having to start from scratch on the period itself. A director should be particularly well versed in the visual arts through the ages. They provide the insights into the life of the past that are most likely to aid a director. For example, I collect old theatrical prints. When I directed *The Way of the World*, I needed information regarding men wearing their hats indoors. A look at a print from the original production of another play by the same author, *The Old Batchelor*, gave me my answer: some did and some did not. Learning has been defined as knowing where to find the information. A director must be knowledgeable enough to know where to go *quickly* for his information.

A would-be director should learn as much as he can about all the equipment that is used in the theater. It is also a great advantage to know something of music. It is not enough to be aware that a woodwind is drowning out certain lyrics. He should be able to tell the musical director whether it is an oboe or a clarinet. He also needs to know enough to stage singers in musically advantageous positions.

For someone who wishes to be a professional director, there are advantages in studying at a university that has a directing program. On campus it is possible to acquire practical experience in directing without the financial pressures of the marketplace. Some universities offer physical plants that are unequaled anywhere and have ample budgets for experimentation. They can also give you the opportunity for practical work with equipment that union regulations would bar you from in the professional world.

The problem is that many college drama departments exist in a vacuum and have no contact with the outside world, although those located in a metropolis are not quite so insular. The professionally oriented student should research the department of his choice carefully to make sure that he is going to get what he is looking for. He should also ascertain whether there is someone teaching in his field whose knowledge has been acquired by experience rather than ''by the book'' (usually Alexander Dean's). There are some good directors in the universities, but you have to seek them out.

This raises the whole question of whether art can be taught. I do not believe that anyone can be taught to be an artist. If someone has a natural aptitude for creative work, then that person can be helped to become much better at it. One can only hope that if the area of interest is directing, he or she will find a teacher who helps to develop the student's way of doing it rather than imposing his or someone else's method on them. The right way to direct is the way that works for each director in the given situation.

I suspect that many of us begin our directing careers by imitating the style of someone whose work we have admired. I certainly did. I became aware of this after a rehearsal of my first professional production. The leading lady was the beautiful British actress, Katherine Blake. She told me that I reminded her of a director she had worked with in England named Glen Byam Shaw. He had been the director who helped me most when I was a student at the Old Vic School, and it was only then that I realized I had been unconsciously copying his style. I am amused now when I notice some of my students imitating me.

The realities of directing are diverse. At the one extreme there are productions where the director is a little more than a traffic cop and on the other there are fantastically rewarding creative experiences. The most successful directors, though not necessarily the best, are likely to be those who can function in the largest variety of circumstances.

The role of the stage director is sometimes decried. I have noticed that the people who seem to think the least of him are those who benefit from him most: bad actors and indifferent playwrights. The best way for the layman to appreciate the contribution of a director is to attend a festival where the same company, under different directors, is appearing in a repertory of plays. Any one of the Stratfords will do very well. You will see the same actors in plays by the same author in the same theater. Ask yourself why those same actors can be excellent in one production and weak in another.

When I was at the University of Washington the B.F.A. program there was above average and their productions usually reflected this fact. When the veteran director Reginald Denham was brought from New York City to direct them in *You Never Can Tell*, a miracle took place. They were no longer good students; they had become young professionals.

It takes a great deal of self-confidence to be a director. You cannot stage a play unless you can convince people that you know what you are doing. On the other hand, I have never met a good director who did not have a genuine sense of humility about what he did. It is a good idea to remind oneself that plays have been put on without us. We, however, cannot be independent of the words of the author, the actors to perform them, and the audience to watch and listen.

Before Stravinsky composed *Apollon Musagète* he asked for the exact performance conditions from the lady who commissioned the ballet. He explained: "The more constraints one imposes, the more one frees oneself. And the arbitrariness of the constraint serves only to obtain precision of executions." Although I know of no stage director whose creativity is equal to that of Stravinsky, I think that his words are directly applicable to our work. The challenge of it and the fun of it (and, thank God, it often is fun) is making all the disparate elements come together into something that is both unified and beautiful.

One of the things that directors say is that they never do a play unless it really excites them. From some of the work I have seen, I feel that many of them must be very excitable. In the course of earning to support my dependents, I have undertaken a number of projects that did not initially "excite" me. These include some of my most successful productions. On the other hand, I have some-times been less than happy with my work on plays that I was absolutely thrilled to be doing, simply because I allowed my enthusiasm to sway my objectivity. This is most likely to happen when one is emotionally and intellectually attracted to the philosophy of the play.

With the economic slump into which this country has plunged at the time of writing, enthusiasm for the art is about all that many theater artists have to sustain themselves. In New York City that "Fabulous Invalid" is looking more like a geriatric case every day.

Any honest book on directing requires a sobering look at the economics of the profession; if there is a harder way of earning a living, I do not know of it. I am not just speaking of the onerous nature of the duties but of the limited opportunities for practicing the craft at all. Just look at the simple statistic that the average play will offer around a dozen jobs for actors but only one for a director.

If you direct and choreograph another *Fiddler on the Roof*, you may well end up with a million dollars. A more typical Broadway assignment would be a new play. A Society of Stage Directors and Choreographers spokesman told me that the average fee for this is now $5,000 (which is $1,250 over that union's minimum) plus a royalty of 2 percent of the weekly gross (this is .5 percent over minimum) for the length of the run. The run would usually be four weeks out of town and two weeks in New York, including previews. Using grosses from *Variety* I have arrived at an average gross for this six weeks as $21,600, so your 2 percent will yield you a total of $2,592. A per diem should take care of most of your out-of-town living expenses, depending on your tastes, but you can no longer show any profit on these expenses. Your grand total for the assignment is therefore $7,592.*

To earn this sum you would have to spend at least three months on casting, meetings with the author, your own preparation, and all the other things I have described in this book. Your rehearsal period is likely to last three weeks and we have already taken care of the further six weeks with which you are fully involved. It is not a lot of money for nearly half a year of concentrated work. I made the "typical" assignment a "flop" because most plays that come to Broadway, except the British imports, close at the end of the week in which they have their press opening.

If you are not an established director, your fee is likely to be S.S.D.C. minimum, which would bring down your total for this hypothetical job, with the royalties at minimum, to $5,694. This is Broadway, the Big Time! And you will probably wait until next season for your next job.

Obviously the reason people take this kind of gamble is that if the show is a hit, you can get very rich indeed. Some plays have as many as three road companies out at the same time and if you do the London production as well, you will even be able to afford beef for your family.

Since the Equity strike of 1970, off-Broadway has virtually disappeared. There are so few fully professional productions now that I will do no more than quote the Society of Stage Directors and Choreographers minimum fee for directing: $750. Royalties are from $30 a week to 2 percent of the gross, depending on the box office potential. The amount of time involved is almost as much as Broadway, so nobody is likely to do one of these productions for

---

*The figures quoted are those current at the time of writing. There are usually annual increases for scale, but these rarely keep up with actual inflation. The costs of lodgings in stock have been especially lethal.

any reason that has to do with money. But off-Broadway remains the best place for a director to be "discovered" if he has Broadway ambitions.

Stock, as I have already said, comes under Actors Equity and the payments are made in weekly salaries. Scale for a play, when you just direct a single one, is $425; and for a musical it is $545. After the show has played for two weeks the director is entitled to a royalty of $60 a week. As many stock theaters take in higher grosses than Broadway (the Saint Louis Municipal Opera can go over $300,000 per week), this royalty arrangement compares quite unfavorably with those made by the Society of Stage Directors and Choreographers. A friend of mine who produces musical stock told me that last summer he had to pay a director a royalty of $1,200 for each week that a certain musical played his theater, simply because it was a pre-Broadway show and not a stock production. The director did not even have to show up to do the necessary restaging.

The dinner theaters come under Equity. This is an expanding field, but it tends to be one in which the producers frequently do the directing themselves. The free-lance rates vary from the rather fey designation "petite" (presumably a reference to the size of the theater rather than the physique of the director) scale $225 to a top of $375 for plays. The director's minimum for a big dinner theater is only $527.50 for a musical.

A major form of free-lance activity for the director is regional theater. The minimum pay scale varies from $2,500 in a "Class A" theater for a rehearsal period not exceeding eight weeks to $750 for three weeks' rehearsal in a "Class C" operation. The letters have nothing to do with quality; the designations are based on the box office potential. The Guthrie Theater in Minneapolis and the Mark Taper Forum in Los Angeles are Class A, whereas the Long Wharf and the Hartford Stage Company are Class C. Obviously, you do not have to work for scale. I have only once; but it is far harder to bargain with regional theaters than Broadway or stock producers because these theaters often operate on minute budgets. So if you want to do the superior plays that they tend to present, you have to make the financial sacrifice as well as live away from home for the rehearsal period.

An artistic director of a regional theater may earn anything between $12,000 and $25,000 a year. I believe there are a couple who receive even more, but most of them are closer to the lower figure. In other words, the man or woman who is the theatrical leader of the community is likely to earn less than a garage mechanic. With administrative responsibilities, board meetings to attend, Elks club luncheons to speak at—to say nothing of the actual business of putting on the shows—a twelve-hour day is the average. It is little wonder that the survival rate in these positions is so low.

The obvious question is, How does the average director survive? The answer is: With difficulty. Some years ago I was told that there was an establishment on Park Avenue which was patronized by ladies of means in search of sexual gratification. My informant went on to tell me that he knew of two Broadway directors who worked there between shows. Whether or not this story is true is unimportant; what is significant is that it was told at all.

The most common method for directors to augment their income is teaching. Every fall one can see advertisements in the press for acting classes taught by well-known directors. The faculties for most of the professional schools in New York City consist largely of directors who work there part-time. Those who have a degree, and a few who do not, teach in universities, where the salaries are generally higher than in conservatories.

Many directors are also actors on the side (as opposed to actors who do a bit of directing on the side). Some are writers, and many end up in executive positions in film and television. I know of one director who supported himself as a painter during a two-year period of unemployment; two others are interior decorators; another reads books for the blind; and several have married well.

Directors in the United States go through periods of being in constant demand and then disappear from sight. In New York it seems as if a handful of people are directing everything—the only change from season to season is the *composition* of this handful.

Despite the enormous unemployment in the field, there are always opportunities for new talent to assert itself. Two of the 1973 season's "hot" directors, A. J. Antoon and Jeff Bleckner, were both recent graduates from Yale who had important assignments, first at the Public Theater and then on Broadway.

My advice to anyone who considers himself ready to direct, but does not have access to the current theatrical czar, Joseph Papp, would be as follows. Find a medium-sized city that does not have a professional theater. Try to find employment there in a related field: a radio station, entertainment section of the local paper, high school drama teacher, or, better still, paid director of a community theater. From this vantage point start your own group at the grass roots level. It is an uphill fight, but it has been done before and will be done more and more in the future. Good theater is no longer exclusively Broadway or West End; it is where it is being done, whether it is Pat Galloway playing *The Duchess of Malfi* at Stratford, Ontario, or Timothy Bottoms as Romeo on the campus of Santa Barbara High School.

In the past people were often terrified of "getting lost out of town." If you are doing exciting work in Spider's Breath, North Dakota, the word will travel fast. You are far more likely to "get lost" sitting in a cold-water flat in Greenwich Village waiting for the phone to ring.

As one of the lucky few who has been able to earn a living in his chosen occupation for twenty-five years, I admit to bias, but I am glad I was not put off the theater by all the dire warnings I received before I started. I write in the knowledge that no young director worth his salt will be unduly discouraged by a brief look at the director's facts of life. The only valid reason for going into the theater is that you love it. You may get rich and famous along the way, but if those are your primary aims, you had better try politics or organized crime.